AMERICA'S BLUNDERS, WONDERS, AND WASTE

Bobby Berry
CHIEF MASTER SERGEANT, U.S. AIR FORCE, RETIRED
(AUTHOR OF HOBOKEN, THE LAND OF PLENTY)

Author's Tranquility Press
Marietta, Georgia

Copyright © 2022 by Bobby Berry

All rights reserved. No part of this publication may be reproduced, distributed, or transmitted in any form or by any means, including photocopying, recording, or other electronic or mechanical methods, without the prior written permission of the publisher, except in the case of brief quotations embodied in critical reviews and certain other noncommercial uses permitted by copyright law. For permission requests, write to the publisher, addressed "Attention: Permissions Coordinator," at the address below.

Bobby Berry/Author's Tranquility Press
2706 Station Club Drive SW
Marietta, GA 30060
www.authorstranquilitypress.com

Ordering Information:
Quantity sales. Special discounts are available on quantity purchases by corporations, associations, and others. For details, contact the "Special Sales Department" at the address above.

America's Blunders, Wonders, and Waste/Bobby Berry
Paperback: 978-1-958554-13-5
eBook: 978-1-958554-14-2

Contents

DEDICATION 4
INTRODUCTION 6
CHAPTER 1 11
CHAPTER 2 37
CHAPTER 3 41
CHAPTER 4 66
CHAPTER 5 74
CHAPTER 6 86
CHAPTER 7 100
CHAPTER 8 106
CHAPTER 9 117
CHAPTER 10 122
CHAPTER 11 132

DEDICATION

This book is dedicated to anyone who ever served in the military, and especially military combat, regardless of the conflict; and to those who returned disabled, and especially those who did not return. And, let us never forget the American tax payer, who continually and unknowingly, contributed <u>trillions upon trillions of dollars to Uncle Sam's bank account</u>; a bank account that no longer exists. Well, if you had a bank account and the bank kept requesting that you stop writing checks because you are broke, would you have a bank account? We'll get back in the black; I have full confidence in America, but perhaps not until 2026. At the writing of this book, the year is 2020, with continued on writing on 4/24/2021. Maybe I'll finish this someday.

First, let's first go down the path of government debt. The government will be paying for our recent Iraq and Afghanistan conflicts alone for the next <u>100 YEARS! ARE YOU KIDDING ME</u>? 100 years?

An analysis by the Associated Press revealed that the government <u>is still making monthly payments</u> to <u>relatives</u> of <u>Civil War veterans; over 150 years after the conflict had ended</u>! We need to pay <u>$40 billion a year</u> to compensate veterans and survivors from the **1898 (Spanish-American War)** through World War I and II, the Korean War, the Vietnam War, the **two Iraq campaigns** and **the Afghanistan conflict**, and these costs continue to rise rapidly. The government has spent more than **$270 Billion in payments to disabled veterans, wartime veterans and their survivors since 1970**. The costliest of all these wars was **The Vietnam War**. Verification of this data can be obtained from the **Freedom of Information Act** in much more detail. I wish someone could tell me what we have gained by our involvement in all but WWI and WWII. WWII caused us to fight to survive; nothing more.

INTRODUCTION

While this book represents a brief but candid military autobiography of the author; a more important purpose, however, is to provide a characterization of <u>"Blunders"</u> that continue to occur in the military and the government today; and that have occurred in the past. There are also some <u>"Wonders"</u> however, that I shall discuss along the way. I label those <u>'good things' as the Wonders</u>. The main wonders of WWI and WWII were that <u>we won those wars</u>! We didn't win in Korea or Vietnam, or any other place since, and I fear that we are going to find ourselves at war back in Korea, and I pray that I am wrong. At the beginning of the writing of this book in 2020, I said, "If President Trump has anything to do with Korea, I believe he can keep the peace with them." Well, he did just that! Now that Sleepy Joe Biden is at the helm, anything can happen that will not be a benefit to the U.S., and I say that because it doesn't seem like he has his total faculty when he speaks. When you lose your faculties, you are powerless. We can't afford a powerless president.

The Middle East would be an ongoing book in itself, however, as those chapters are <u>still in progress</u>! These portrayals are presented here as facts, and in no way, do they represent unfounded negativity by the author! If the facts appear rather negative, then it's only because they were negative. I would also like it to be known that I am proud of serving my country for over 27 years in the United States Air Force, where I was awarded the Bronze Star in Vietnam. And, let it be known that I love my country, care about my country, and will always stand ready to serve it; so, don't let all the negativity you are about to read portray anything else as concerns my attitude toward America.

Next, I'll begin with the time frame of 1968 and 1969, which was the hottest time of the Vietnam War. The accounts I shall portray are factual and accurate. I have firsthand knowledge of events I shall be discussing from this time frame; since I was serving in Vietnam during the period portrayed. This book shall also be a depiction of **military stupidity** along the way, both before and after the unpopular war of Vietnam. At this point, a good question might be, why the hell I am dealing with such a controversial subject that has no apparent remedies? Well, let's see where this goes and perhaps than you, as a reader, can arrive at your own conclusions. My mission is to get most people who read this, to realize that our government, as concerns the military should **pull their heads out of the sand**, and realize that we have now, and have had in the past, numerous people representing this country, who don't have enough sense to come out of the rain! While it's too late to do anything about that; **let this book be a guide to how and whom we vote for in the future.** But I know it won't!

Upon my return from Vietnam in 1969, my teenage nephews in California questioned my loyalty to the United States for fighting in what was called, "**An Unjust War**". It was also a time when Jane Fonda surprisingly declared that the United States was wrong for fighting this "unjust war". Hanoi Jane's comments, although having some merit, were very untimely while our boys were being killed; the final tally being over 56,000. I am going to convey in this book, things that most uninformed Americans did not know, because the U.S. Government seemed oblivious to them as well, as I discovered was the case most of the time throughout my 27 years of Service in the U.S. Air Force. But I hung in there!

Back to Jane Fonda; I give her credit for having the balls to expose a lot of the bull shit that was happening at the risk of her being condemned for the rest of her life; which she was! She certainly didn't have to do it for fame or money; so, what was her motive? While this may be hard to accept for the Jane Fonda haters; she had one motive. She knew that if she used her celebrity to denounce the war we finally lost, hell yes; we lost it, people would pay attention! Believe it or not, her motive was pure patriotism! She wanted our boys out of Vietnam; no more, no less. History later proved how right she was. Most of the Fonda haters are not even aware of some of her comments. Contrary to popular belief, she never condemned the fighting man, directly or indirectly in any way; as her condemnation was directed at the United States for their usual butting into other people's dirty linen. This was a civil war and none of our business. On Jane Fonda, although I believed her motive was one of patriotism, I nevertheless condemn the timing of it and, especially her doing it at the Hanoi Hilton

<u>where our prisoners were housed</u>; of all places! She could have condemned the damn war like every citizen in America was doing, right here in America! Had she done that, guess what; she would have been a hero, which is typical American bull shit! To prove my point, famous actresses <u>Jean Simmons</u>, and <u>Donna Reed</u>, said <u>the very same things</u> that Jane said, but they said it from U.S. soil. They go down in history as true patriots. God, what is wrong with us? Boy, political correctness has always had us by the balls, and does it ever get worse! And according to eye witness prisoners, Jane Fonda never turned the notes that were handed to her by prisoners over to the North Vietnamese, as alleged! This was typical news distortion for sensationalism, and that is what is so corrupt about the mainstream media; even today. Especially today! Eyewitnesses came forward and indicated that she did not hand them the notes, yet this was ignored by the media because it perpetrated the ongoing hate for Jane that had been brewing. In the past 50 years, Freedom of the Press has gone to extremes. They now seem to be free to print anything, whether true or false. Now, this so-called News Freedom means, <u>forget the actual news, and express the station's views!</u> Fortunately, some of the general public are finally wise to these distortions and have discovered that between the three or the four major news media, an event can be reported in ways that either favor or disfavor people, regardless of whether or not the information is true. The FCC publishes specific rules and guidelines related to news hoaxes and distortions, and bars a licensee from "Knowingly Broadcasting False Information." Just six days after Donald Trump's first Tweet, the FCC Chairman, Ajith Pai, said his agency cannot

revoke the license of a broadcaster based on the content of a particular newscast, and cited First Amendment protections of the press. The bottom line here is, the FCC is a paper tiger with no teeth these days, unlike the WWII years when they would almost suspend a license if you sneezed. So, what we have now is simply that they will not interfere with DISTORTED, OVER DRAMATIZED, OR STORIES COVERED INADEQUATELY, simply because they feel that interference would be inconsistent with the Constitution because they then opine that "this would be an act of replacing a journalist's judgment of a licensee with a judgment of their own (whatever the hell that means)! There is an old wise saying that goes like this, "Believe nothing you hear and only half of what you see!" In today's world, there are two major lies; the media, and the Polls, and there is still a lot of old-timers out there who believe that "if it is in the Newspaper, it has to be true".

CHAPTER 1

While, as you read this book, you may feel that I am bitter over my twenty-seven + years of military service; such a conclusion, however, would be totally false. On the contrary, I am extremely proud of my service and especially my country, and did what a professional soldier was supposed to do; follow orders without question. Hopefully, military men and women are still allowed <u>to love their country</u>, <u>serve their country</u>, and at the same time, <u>not be happy with the idiots</u> who try to write the words to music, when they don't even know the melody! I could write a separate book on all the blunders created by Generals during America's wars. The blunders that cost the vast loss of lives of our troops, not commensurate with the desired outcome of the battle objective. I have always pondered how the battle philosophies might have changed if the planners who approved the plan had to be in the middle of the battle <u>with their asses on the line</u>! Funny; with that scenario, I keep seeing an entirely different approach to the battle plan, and; <u>I see much fewer casualties</u>. <u>Isn't that amazing?</u> Am I wrong? I think all the soldiers should be on a hill a mile from the battlefield with huge binoculars watching the Generals in hand-to-hand combat! After all, this is what Generals do, and they get a damn chest full of ribbons for watching. Although a screwball and a psychotic, at least General George Patton, would fit the category of **putting his ass closer** to the line for his battle plan. Well, not really, as he never got up in the tank during the combating drive, but posed in them moving along after the battle was over. Kind of a Hollywood thing. Good old glory-seeking George; he was a rare bird, yet, a WWII hero. In wars, you must have heroes to brag about, like Generals Eisenhower and Macarthur.

Let's digress and look at some World War II blunders for a moment. The biggest problem during WWII was **logistics**! The supply train (Red Ball Express) had to stop carrying larger caliber artillery since **the priority was fuel**. What's the good of having fuel if you don't have large-caliber artillery? The priority should have been an **evenly balanced plan** to accommodate, fuel, artillery, the troops, and everything else necessary as a **blend of needs** at the correct time. This will be very difficult for the readers to accept, but battle plans which did not encompass an **evenly balanced plan, logistically**, were missing the boat most of the time. Yes, there will always be casualties in wars, but better planning will cut the loss of life down **monumentally**! Will I be super critical of Generals and the officer corps in the military who continued to blunder and disgrace the country they swore to proudly serve? I feel it my solemn duty to bring it to the front, without distortion. In other words, I'm going to cut the Bull Shit about these kinds of things just like Trump does.

What price should be paid for a battle victory? This was the mindset of the academy graduates as these very things we're taught in the military academies. I do not condemn the cadets who were brainwashed in archaic methods, nor the curriculum they studied. Let's face it; whatever we think we learned from World War I could not be translated to World War II, just as World War II did not help toward winning the wars in Korea or Vietnam. It was the politicians who always wanted an estimate as to the numbers of military personnel that might be lost due to a planned offensive. Washington would go along with the plan of the **offensive**, after the Joint Chiefs would endorse the plan as "<u>FEASABLE</u>", after all, why should they overly endorse a plan and become a scapegoat? This way, Washington had clean hands, the Joint Chiefs had clean hands, and the battle planners, the generals, had clean hands, while the troops in the field became the culprits instead. The Generals in Washington (the Joint Chiefs), and the elected officials were obsessed with things happening quickly, rather than correctly. Unfortunately, the Generals were always underestimating the enemy, which I shall discuss further. Quite too often they did not choose <u>**the best priority; the men, as history, clearly reveals that the men were the second priority**</u> and were treated as expendable units; like bullets! When generals were asked how many casualties they estimated in the planned conflict, they would pull a number out of their asses. <u>**Their lives were never included in that number!**</u> The actual number of casualties was usually 30% higher than their estimates. Why? If they gave high loss estimates, their battle plans would not have been approved! So, like I said, "out of their asses came the numbers". While they had the opportunity to second think the planned offensive with a view toward **fewer casualties**, that subject never surfaced. Their philosophy (taught from their academies) was, that victory will always produce casualties. All the generals were in too much of a hurry to forge ahead like General George Patton. It was a win, win, and win, at whatever the cost of the expendable men. The Germans were greatly outnumbered by a 20 to 1 margin, but they were resilient. One way that the Germans hit back at Patton was, they studied Patton's weaknesses and used them to their advantage. Yes, contrary to popular belief, Patton had weaknesses. One of his biggest combat weaknesses was that **he always neglected to practice economy of force**, allowing the Germans to succeed in counter-attacks against his Army. The economy of Force is better defined as **"NOT OUTRUNNING YOUR SUPPLIES!"** The Germans knew that Patton was a charging bull. Often, they purposely retreated to a point commensurate with a place where they knew Patton would outrun his fuel and ammunition supply. This is when they would pounce on his forces and create tremendous casualties and losses of tanks. Another big mistake of Patton's was when he decided to spread out his Third Army over a vast frontal area believing his army was that strong. His belief was that it would spread strength across a broader area. This backfired on him as it provided a broader, **weaker front**, resulting in **huge casualties and losses of tanks**; a tremendous blunder that never seemed to make the headlines, <u>like the slapping of a private did</u>. Because of Patton's mistakes, Omar Bradley and Eisenhower changed that system to <u>fighting concentrated and tight</u>. Fighting concentrated and tight, while a sound tactic for ground troops, proved to be a <u>disaster</u> for aircraft formations. Eisenhower personally removed these helter-skelter activities of George Patton's military offensives, otherwise, there would be no stopping him. While he won battles, his <u>blunders</u> caused <u>unnecessary casualties</u>. Patton was stubborn enough not to accept the fact that <u>logistics is the key to success in any battle</u>. His "<u>Damn the torpedoes; full speed ahead attitude</u>", was his biggest downfall. He was obsessed with beating Field Marshall Montgomery to an objective location <u>at any cost</u>! I should say, at any cost <u>to his men</u>! It seems that Washington was happy to provide all the accolades they could to assure the American public that Generals like George Patton and Douglas MacArthur were winning the war for us; single-handedly. They were blinded by Patton's miraculous charges to the front, and casualty numbers were never provided to the public during the war, which is best described as, <u>protecting a psychotic</u>! But I have to admit, America needed these kinds of assurances to remain positive about the conduct of the war.

Generals have always calculated the percentage of casualties to expect in an upcoming combat mission, using a standard calculation that had very little validity; the system was referred to by the enlisted men as, "Generals pulling numbers out of their asses." Their inability to accurately tackle the mission commensurate with common sense and regard for the power of the enemy often wound up <u>being the missing element</u>. They were victims of what they learned in their respective academies, so who can we blame for that? I'm not blaming the academies for anything because WWII was unlike WWI in a thousand ways as I previously stated. WWI was the only yardstick they had besides the archaic studies of Hannibal. It has become apparent throughout history, that most Generals and Admirals were <u>victims of habit</u>. Whatever worked last month, or during WWI or WWII should work today. Victories did not come that cheap, however. While it may sound like I am hinging on the brink of <u>armchair quarterbacking</u>; the actual events of WWII and the Vietnam War support downright <u>stupidity</u>, without the aid of my armchair quarterbacking.

Here is a classic example of a General with his <u>headway the hell up his ass</u>; while <u>Washington was oblivious to his methods</u> of accomplishment of the missions he pursued. General Curtis Lemay (then Colonel, and a legend in his own mind), 8th Air Force Commander, ordered <u>daylight bombing</u> in Europe with a <u>tight as possible</u> box formation of B-17s. Washington never questioned it, nor did they seem to pay much attention to <u>60 of 290 B-17s being shot down</u> during the <u>first week of the war from just one mission</u>! Lemay was convinced that enemy fighters would think twice to attack his tight box flying formation, because of all the gun power that existed on the Flying Fortresses. <u>What an idiot</u>! He was also a

General who was opposed to servicemen having an auto racing hobby, yet, he used Military Airlift Aircraft to transport the sports car he raced on occasions at Riverside, California; <u>a very well-kept secret</u>! Back to his genius tactic of <u>close support</u>, this formation made fighter attacks simpler for the enemy, because it was hard to <u>deliberately miss</u> hitting several planes at one pass.

Lemay was a George Armstrong Custer type of eccentric, as his behavior was rather unconventional and slightly strange. When Lemay gave briefings, he made sure that he had his <u>big ugly cigar dangling from his mouth, dripping juice and all</u>, in a gesture of being a tough old bastard; which he was! How do I know this? I was assigned to Strategic Air Command (SAC), where he was Commander for a good portion of my service. There was a situation when he was in a staff car coming through the front gate. The front gate military policeman, immediately recognizing that it was General Lemay because of his flags on the front bumper, and because he recognized that it was Lemay, gave him a wave and a salute to passing through the gate. Lemay had the driver stop the vehicle, went over to the Security Policeman, took his name, and had him reduced in rank for not physically checking his identification, calling it a breach of security. I have personal knowledge of this event because I worked as a Legal Specialist in the JAG OFFICE and knew the person who was screwed. If you want to be a pompous ass hole, or if you wanted to be the King of all ass holes, this would be the <u>blueprint</u> for attaining that goal. If this is not an ass hole, then

God didn't make little green apples, and it doesn't rain in Indianapolis in the summertime! Such a reputation as this did not foster respect from his troops for this general. He demanded respect but didn't have a clue as to how to earn it.

It needs to be remembered that guys like Custer, Patton, and Douglas MacArthur, were not Generals per-say either; <u>they were Gods</u>! They rarely followed military protocol! They designed their own uniforms contrary to written directives which governed the wearing of <u>GOVERNMENT ISSUE UNIFORMS</u>. Wearing an improper uniform for an enlisted man meant, strong disciplinary punishment, including possible loss of rank. This is a great example of an abuse of <u>RHIP</u> (Rank has its privileges)! Patton wore a pearl handle pistol on each hip (he said they were ivory), and MacArthur had a hat designed after British military officer hats. His hat was truly unique; rather good-looking, and was a symbol of who he was, and his long stem corn cob pipe was part of the persona he wanted to portray. During World War II, the only General who did not believe that he was <u>God Like</u> was <u>General Dwight D. Eisenhower</u>, even though <u>he was God-like</u>! His conduct and planning of the war, together with his ability to be an example of great leadership, together with his association with other allied commanders; was flawless. Thank God, we had <u>some</u> high-ranking officers like him and General Omar Bradley. Unlike George Patton, they wanted to <u>win the war</u> and <u>go home</u>, whereas Patton wanted to <u>play war forever</u> to satisfy his ego.

He truly believed that he was born and destined to lead armies. What a nut!

Back to General Lemay (Old Iron Pants as he was called, besides a lot of other names). He single-handedly took on the task of <u>daylight bombing</u>. The British were much smarter, as they volunteered to take the <u>night runs</u>. Lemay was a <u>very brave son of a bitch</u> to take on the risk of daylight bombing, especially since he only <u>FLEW ON A HANDFUL OF THE BOMB RUNS during the end of the war when German Airpower was almost non-existent</u>! When Lemay was in the Pacific after the European operation, he often flew on the runs, but that was because the Japanese Airpower was non-existent at this period, and it was safe to fly. The Brits did more damage with less loss of aircraft compared to the Americans doing less damage with a very <u>unacceptable</u> number of aircraft losses because the <u>American planes rarely got all the way to the target as they were shot down</u> until the P-51 Mustangs began to escort them all the way to the target and back towards the end of the war. Lemay's bombers, using what was known as a 'box formation', gave the results of <u>ONLY 5% OF THE BOMBS HITTING THEIR TARGETS WHILE THE FORTRESSES WERE EASY TARGETS FOR ENEMY FIGHTERS BECAUSE OF LEMAY'S TIGHT FORMATION HORSE SHIT</u>!

The Norden Bombsight was in question for quite a while as to the accuracy, and even with daylight bombing, only 5% of the targets were hit! Not only were the aircraft losses unacceptable;

but **downright disgusting!** Adding to that terrible statistic, it was routine that when twenty B-17s went out for a bomb run, on average, only eight came back! To put it bluntly, that's about **120 human beings**. I suppose that was considered acceptable since we built over 12,000 B-17s for the war effort, so I guess the aircraft were **expendable along with the crews**; but the loss of **SIXTY B-17s FROM JUST ONE BOMB RUN** at Regensburg, Germany, under the command of General Lemay (who, surprisingly, was flying on that mission), was, by far, **one of the biggest blunders of the war**! It is well documented that thousands of young men **died each day**, just to put **a few bombs on very few obscure targets** that were hit at the beginning of the war. In all, 40,000 aircrews were killed during the European conflict. While I can't prove the statistic, I am about to portray; it is my opinion that this number could have, and should have, **been cut by 60%!** So, for what it's worth, my educated guess is, 24,000 fewer deaths of airmen would have been feasible. I guess we all are entitled to our opinions. As this was our first war since WWI, we had no way of determining if such a loss ratio was good or bad for aircraft, so we just **continued to BLUNDER** by continuing to send planes on high-risk missions without fighter support! Fighter support did not happen until toward the end of the war in Europe. Someone woke up and came up with the idea of escorting the bombers, but nobody knows who gets the credit. The range of the P-51 was perfect to escort the bomber when it became available. While Lemay did some good things, those good things were nothing more than **things he was paid to accomplish**. In the military, you didn't get applause for doing what you were supposed to be doing. The only applause you could earn was when you did something **ABOVE AND BEYOND THE CALL OF DUTY**, which only a hand full of Generals earned, and Lemay certainly was not one of them in my opinion, based upon the available air combat statistics. His carpet bombing with incendiaries over Japan, while effective, was not necessarily heroic. At this particular time, Japan had relatively no aircraft left to attack these formations. As commander of Strategic Air Command (SAC), he did develop war plans to attack Russia in the event of war, but here again, he was doing what he was paid to do, and did a credible job at that task.

Here is something to ponder about cigar-chewing Lemay. While he demanded the utmost, unquestioned discipline from his men, he disliked authority above him, especially when it came from the COMMANDER IN CHIEF OF THE ARMED FORCES; THE PRESIDENT OF THE UNITED STATES, NAMELY; PRESIDENT JOHN F. KENNEDY! It is well known and accepted in the military that, to give orders, one must be able to take orders equally well. Lemay did not buy into this scenario! He had his own agenda and argued with Kennedy and the Secretary of Defense with total disregard for their desires. Because of his attitude, he was eventually asked to resign, which thank God, he did. At this point, you, as a reader, should be able to determine what a blowhard ass hole Lemay became, just in case you may have thought he was a hero. It would have been entertaining at best, had Donald Trump been the president at that time period rather than JFK. He would not have been asked to resign, he would have been FIRED! Regardless of one's military rank, it is not necessary to like the President's policies; one just has to follow them, as it only happens to be part of the oath we take!

At one point, during a meeting with the President and the Joint Chiefs, when the President (JFK) indicated that he wanted to avoid a nuclear war with Cuba and how very concerned he was, Lemay boldly interrupted with a smirk on his face and the comment, "<u>In other words, you're in a pretty bad fix at the present time</u>!" Kennedy took immediate offense to this and said, "<u>What did you say</u>"? Lemay repeated with a smirk, "<u>You're in a pretty bad fix ain't you</u>?" Kennedy, being the fox that he was said with a smile, "<u>You're in there right with me general</u>!" It was at this point that Lemay <u>instantly realized</u> that he no longer was God, while <u>FINALLY</u> realizing that he had interrupted <u>God</u>!

Kennedy, upon his entry into the presidency, was shocked at the power of Generals and Admirals in the field <u>who could start a nuclear war if they thought it was necessary</u>. He was upset with how they would make statements to the press which were <u>never</u> supportive of his views, and they asked no one for permission to make press releases because the Generals and Admirals <u>were Gods</u>! Kennedy soon put the kibosh on both loose cannon issues by tying their hands and requiring them to clear all press releases through him for approval. Did this piss off the Gods with the Stars on their collars? I believe we could say "yes" to that question. He also made it clear that no General or Admiral in the field had the authority to start a nuclear conflict under any circumstances, reminding them that such action is an act of war and that only Congress could declare war. MacArthur did not buy into that EITHER until Truman had to relieve him to get his attention as the General was ready to go right on into China. The Joint Chiefs hated JFK as they saw their former power pulled out from under them. Kennedy would often say to his brother Bobby, "<u>These guys with all the Fruit Salad on their chest think they are in control of the President</u>"! It is reported that Bobby would usually answer with, "<u>Damn right, you are in control of them</u>"! Again, how, over time, the Joint Chiefs changed the rules of the ball game by losing sight of their required duty to <u>**ADVISE THE PRESIDENT; AND NOT ARGUE WITH THE PRESIDENT**</u>, was absolutely <u>disgusting</u>! Thank God, the Joint Chiefs now realize that they still come <u>**UNDER**</u> the President, and know that their mission is to <u>**advise the President**</u>, thanks to Kennedy's game change. Immediately after the meeting with the President and the Joint Chiefs, a tape recorder caught the military brass <u>(the Gods)</u> blasting the commander in chief, as <u>Marine Commandant David Shoup</u> said to Lemay, "<u>You pulled the rug right out from under him, didn't you! Somebody needs to keep them from doing the goddamn thing piecemeal; this is our</u>

problem, not theirs! You go in there friggin around with missiles; you're screwed...do it right and quit friggin around!"

Having heard this, Kennedy told his longtime aide Kenny O'Donnell, "If we do what they want us to do, none of us will be alive later to tell them that they were wrong". Even though Kennedy could get Khrushchev to back down without nuclear intervention, it pissed off the joint chiefs to no end, as they were proven wrong. They refused to recognize Kennedy's victory and said some underhanded things about his Cuban victory. General Lemay portrayed the missile crisis that Kennedy solved as, "The greatest defeat in our history". Admiral George Anderson, the Navy Chief of Staff declared, "We have been had". Kennedy was not only shocked by their remarks, but deeply hurt by the fact that they were not willing to see success in the settlement for the United States and the world without the intervention of war. If this does not support my personal feelings that certain high-ranking officers just don't know how to limit their alleged power, then I don't know what will. Through their military careers, as they go through the ranks and finally attain the stars on their shoulders, they experience the power they had not experienced at even the full Colonel rank. After years in the general ranks, they lose themselves in a fantasy dream that they, in fact, have power that no other human being possesses. During President Trump's presidency, he appointed several generals to high posts, relying on their vast military experiences of command, only to find out that generals were totally out of touch with the real civilian world. They obviously were not the best of choices as it later turned out, and President Trump had the balls to tell them, "You're fired!"

The negative feeling toward President Kennedy was also expressed clearly by the Chairman of the Joint Chiefs, <u>Lyman Lemnitzer</u>, who commented, <u>"Here is a President who has no military experience at all, except as a Patrol Boat Skipper"</u>! Can you believe this sort of shit from our high-ranking idiots? But through it all, guess what; many high-ranking officers still act and feel God Like, so not much has changed, <u>but does require drastic change!</u> The question is, when will this <u>INSUBORDINATION</u> end?

Let's discuss another disgraceful incident as concerned General Petraeus. After lying and lying, and lying, he finally pleaded guilty to <u>giving classified journals</u> to, guess who? <u>HIS FRIGGIN MISTRESS!!!!!!!!</u> He admitted that he gave her eight handwritten journals containing <u>highly classified information</u> about secret operations and <u>the friggin identities of covert officers in 2011,</u> and then lied about it to the FBI. Excuse me for my overuse of the word friggin. I use it to avoid the other "F" word, which may slip out now and then for emphasis. Because of his former status as CIA Chief, guess what; <u>No prison time, even though he should have been charged with obstruction of justice and lying to the FBI;</u>

<u>two damn felony federal offenses, together with major security breaches</u>! He did get somewhat of a sanction with two years' probation and a $100,000 fine for sharing classified government information with his lover/biographer, Paula Broadwell.

What he was charged with carries a one-year maximum prison sentence. According to the great David Petraeus, "<u>America is making a comeback</u>". When he was <u>a hero four-star general</u>, he wore his ten rows of <u>hero fruit salad</u> from his shoulder down to his ass hole! These ribbons, as is the case for a great number of high-ranking officers were, in actuality; <u>attendance ribbons</u>, not hero ribbons! A private equity firm hired Petraeus to write about, '<u>How America is Making a Comeback</u>'. Give me a break! Since his return to civilian life, he was associated with CUNY (The City University of New York). Protestors at that university created quite a ruckus over him being at the university, to re-teach a course called, "Are we on the Threshold of the North American Decade?" He also joined Harvard Kennedy School, where he met his mistress in 2006, as a non-resident senior fellow. This hero had also taught at USC in Los Angeles, where he lectured about international relations and mentored student-veterans and Trojans participating in ROTC. You see, he brings his <u>four-star General Head</u> with him wherever he goes! What a disgrace he is to the American fighting man, and to the <u>ever-diminishing honor</u> of the officer corps. His buddy, <u>General John Allen</u>, was also under heavy suspicion as well for having potentially inappropriate communications with a woman named, Jill Kelley. He was supposed to become the successor to Petraeus, which sounds like an easy transition going from one loser to another.

What the hell is it with these **TIN GODS THAT WE CALL GENERALS AND ADMIRALS**? Shit, it goes all the way back to **General Benedict Arnold** who became the **first traitor** in American history. He may very well head the list of the number one all-time disgraced military generals.

Sorry, but we can't hide good old **Douglas MacArthur** under the rug, however. For all of the good accomplishments he achieved, he nevertheless came close to causing a war with China due to his **insubordinate behavior** by outright defiance of an American president. His defiance of President Truman ranks as **the greatest act of outright defiance** of an American president, by a general of the armed forces.

Then going back further in time there was **General George B. McClellan**, replaced by Abe Lincoln who had to fire him for his failure to push hard against the Confederacy, during a very defining moment of the Civil War. Then he was replaced by the bumbling and incompetent **General Ambrose Burnside**, who had to be removed in favor of **General Joseph Hooker**. Then there was **General William Hull** who, while defending Michigan and attacking in Canada, and due to his poor planned invasion, was forced to retreat to Detroit where he surrendered without a fight. For this, he was court-martialed and convicted of cowardice and neglect of duty. He received a death sentence which President James Madison remitted. Then there was General Thomas Algeo Rowley of Civil War times who was removed for his constant drunkenness and disobeyance of orders. Another disobeying general!

During the early writings of this book, Secretary of Defense Ash Carter had fired a three-star general for 'allegations of misconduct'. The general is his Senior Military Assistant, Lieutenant General Ron Lewis. The misconduct, reportedly, is for an allegation of an "improper relationship." The situation was in the hands of the Inspector General to determine all the facts. Nothing happened to him! When will this shit with Generals and Admirals subside? One thing is sure, it appears that, subject to popular belief, high-ranking officers do like sex. There are over 15 more generals which I shall let go for now, who were ousted for guess what? DISOBEDEYANCE OF ORDERS. Misconduct and disobedience of orders have been, and is, rampant, as concerns the conduct of high-ranking officers. Coming from the enlisted ranks, and having been a 27+ year Air Force Chief Master Sergeant, it becomes rather difficult for me to understand these shameful acts of disobedience of orders and sexual misconduct.

So, I must ask, am I picking on high-ranking officers, or do they deserve their own fame without my help? I believe that the four years of brainwashing at their respective academies causes their defiance, as it is instilled that they will **someday become Tin Gods**! I have been informed by a close friend and former Naval Officer, that changes for the good have been taking place in the academies; or at least Annapolis. I was very glad to hear that. The power of Generals and Admirals must become rather mind-boggling for them and confusing, especially when they seem to have extreme difficulty <u>dealing with orders from leaders above them</u>.

They are, in essence, order givers; **not order takers!** I believe that the defiance of the Commander in Chief is the quintessential example of their unruly mindset. They are not war stoppers, they seem to love conflict in war, because that's when their promotions flourish and when their chests become full of ribbons. Let me be fair about all this dirt. <u>There surely are numerous high-ranking officers who do not fall under these categories, and who, with dignity and respect, honor the rank they possess, and I proudly salute those who fall under this category.</u>

While I have already discussed **blow-hard** Lemay, I might add that he proved his belligerence **further and finally**, by becoming a vice-presidential candidate for the worst segregationist and bigot in history; Governor George Wallace.

Lemay definitely had a screw loose somewhere, and this act proved my theory.

As to the disgrace of General Petraeus, A Taliban spokesman, Qazi Yousuf Ahmadi stated, "I can say that this shows how shameless all the American troops are, starting from the top commander down to the soldiers, as having unlawful relations with a woman is very normal in America."

This statement personally burns my friggin ass! Thank you, Mr. Petraeus; you are not worthy of being called General Petraeus even though you still receive a healthy yearly military pension as a friggin four-star general! And as for you, Mr. Ahmadi, at least we don't use animals for our shameless behavior!

Have you ever noticed that most high rankers, like Lemay, usually have nine friggin rows of ribbons on their chest? (In the military, we call these ribbons, fruit salad). It certainly makes them look like heroes. Well, I only have four rows of ribbons, but mine were earned by serving in those combat areas, not just flying in, calling the visit a one-day inspection, and getting a ribbon for being in that theatre of operation for twenty-four hours. You see, theatre commanders can fly in and out of any place and call those fly-ins INSPECTIONS! 95% of the vast number of ribbons you see on high-ranking officers are actually, ATTENDANCE MEDALS! YES, FRIGGIN ATTENDANCE MEDALS! I'm sorry, I probably should not have revealed that military secret. This is exactly how high-ranking Officers get a chest full of ribbons; I mean a friggin chest full! Isn't that disgusting? I spent 365 days in a combat zone to receive three medals for my service in the war zone, and one Bronze Star (None of which were attendance medals), while one-star and two-star generals were flying in and out to visit the MACV commander, General Westmoreland, for one day, entitling them to three more service medals for their chest. Enlisted men have no way to compete with that scenario! Eisenhower only had the same number of rows of ribbons as I had, because he was preoccupied with the planning of the war in Europe, rather than flying in and out of combat zones to pad his chest with phony fruit salad. Well, now you have learned how higher-ranking officers EARN all those ribbons. Not very heroic, is it? By the way, bad blunders are usually rewarded in the military. To prove it; Lemay came back from being a full Colonel at the beginning of the war, to a four-star general! Enlisted returning men were lucky to have been promoted one to two grades, rather than four grades like the Colonels who made four-star Generals. What more proof is needed for Rank has its privileges?

Here is a point of interest. During WWII, General George Patton was awarded two Distinguished Service Crosses, three Distinguished Service Medals, two Silver Stars, The Legion of Merit, the Bronze Star, and the Purple Heart which he received for a leg wound in World War I. Why didn't his men in combat in the field get two Distinguished Service Crosses, three Distinguished Service medals, two Silver Stars, The Legion of Merit, and the Bronze Star for their involvement in the same conflicts? Because Patton put all the paperwork forward for his decorations, which he received, but none for his men.

<u>Lunie Toons Patton</u> believed in reincarnation. He claimed, in other lives, he was a Roman Legionnaire. He believed that after his death, he would return to once again lead armies into battle. It took him five years to complete West Point rather than the normal four years it takes because he had to repeat his first year. Now, visualize this great general, high on his perch about a mile away from the combat area, with his binoculars watching the troops in combat, **<u>and watching them get blown to pieces</u>**! True, the battle plan was his (which was often the problem), but his men put **<u>their asses on the line</u>**! Therefore, **<u>I have to ask</u>,** why shouldn't they **<u>have every damn ribbon on their chest that PATTON had during World War II?</u>** You'll never see enlisted troops with nine rows of ribbons on their chest because only high-ranking officers pick and choose their awards! Think about it! **<u>What did Patton do that exceeded the tasks of his men dying in the field of combat?</u>** These are the many things that have caused me to lose respect for the officer corps. In the eyes of most enlisted men; **<u>most officers have no credibility</u>**! I truly wish we could feel

differently since these are the bastards who are supposed to lead us as well as see to our needs.

How America continues to thrive in the world as a power, despite bad politics and unscrupulous and incapable high-ranking officers, has, and always will, amaze me! Technically, General Lemay should have been asked to resign his commission during WWII for the loss of an average of 300 men a day, <u>due to his hair brain close formation tactic!</u> In my opinion, <u>he got away with murder!</u> President Kennedy did ask him to resign during the Cuban Crisis for his apparent extremely bad attitude in following the game plan. Fortunately, he did resign. President Trump would have said, "Hey lard ass, you're fired!" However, his success in Japan with the incendiary carpet-bombing kind of <u>disguised</u> his inadequacies of the European Theatre. But again, you get paid for what you are supposed to accomplish.

Now Let's go to Pearl Harbor for another example of a General ordering a tight ground formation of aircraft in the interest of precluding <u>ground sabotage</u>; while providing an easy target for the Japanese Zeroes, as all 73 planes on the ground at Wheeler and Hickam Air Bases were easily <u>destroyed in just two passes</u>; representing another example of tight formations which proved disastrous. His name was <u>GENERAL WALTER SHORT.</u> After the attack on Pearl Harbor, Short was ordered back to Washington by Army Chief of Staff, George C. Marshall. It's not like we didn't know that if America was attacked, it would happen at Pearl Harbor and the Japanese would be the attackers, as predicted in the 1930s by General Billy Mitchell. We also knew that faulty negotiations were taking place in Washington with Japan as a prelude to war. **Admiral Kimmel** was another Pearl Harbor freak who had to be relieved by FDR after the attack on Pearl Harbor, for having his head up his ass so far, **that he never even heard the air raid siren**! Kimmel, it was said, was a creature of habit. He was not innovative and always continued to do what he had always done. But let's face it, none of our Commanders were combat experienced at this point of the war. Kimmel lacked imagination and insight **and represented the typical floundering officer I continue to discuss**. And, in fairness, I must again reiterate that all officers were not in this category. His lackadaisical attitude was like a disease that permeated down to the men at Pearl Harbor. **What the hell do they teach at West Point and the Naval Academy?** I'll tell you what they teach. **TRADITION, TRADITION, TRADITION**! The **same shit** they taught when George Armstrong Custer and Ulysses S. Grant **finished dead last in their class**! There are over a hundred more blunders that would boggle one's mind, but this book will not cover them all. It will, however, cover the period shown at the beginning of this text, together with a few other periods which will depict the **waste of resources and misdirection of Generals that I have witnessed, specifically; throughout my career**. On with **the facts**.

It was once said, "<u>We have to be critical of military blunders if we hope to avoid</u> <u>repeating the mistakes of the past</u>". This is exactly why I am on the attack! Apparently, we <u>learned nothing</u> from the blunders of World Wars I or II, because our floundering continued through Korea and Vietnam. The Middle East is another story, and perhaps a book in itself!

History clearly reveals the many blunders of World War II; blunders which undoubtedly were direct causes of <u>UNNECESSARY CASUALTIES.</u> The Germans were certainly aware of our military academy studies. They knew that our graduates and future leaders studied battles of Alexander the Great, Hannibal, William the conqueror, and other historic battles, and how their thinking was affected by these studies. Most of our foot soldier's leaders all felt that football tactics often were appropriate for battle strategy. The Germans used all that knowledge to determine whether a general was <u>trapped by archaic historic battles,</u> or whether he was an <u>innovative, unpredictable bastard!</u>

Here is a naval blunder that did not cause the unnecessary loss of life, but instead, revealed a decision that backfired on <u>Admiral William 'Bull' Halsey,</u> while he used a tactic of <u>fixed principal</u> qualifying him as <u>a trapped strategist of archaic battle history</u>! In the face of two Japanese naval forces, his decision not to divide the fleet (known as the <u>principal of mass</u>) caused the entire enormous American

Naval force to be prepared to fight a <u>DECOY JAPANESE FLEET</u>; not a big thing because a division of the fleet would still have left Halsey superior to both Japanese forces. But he was predictable because he was a creature of habit, and of course, this was also his first war. As the war ensued, he lost many of his old habits; it seemed, breaking from traditional failures and accomplishing valuable successes.

What mistakes did the United States make at the outset of WWII? While we should have joined France and England to attack Germany after they invaded Poland; we did not!

A huge error! Blame this error on Congress who, for political promises and for the sake of politicians seeking re-election, kept a blind eye as to what the ramifications might be while sitting on their hands. Congress made it plain to Roosevelt that they were not interested in declaring war in Europe, even though they knew that war would be inevitable. They preferred that we pay the price as we did at Pearl Harbor first before they would favor a declaration of war, which kept their hands squeaky clean. Accordingly, Roosevelt needed a reason to enter the war which he sorely wanted to do, to help England sooner, as they were going down the tubes! Pearl Harbor did the trick, and Hitler declaring war on the U.S. gave us the ability to aid England immediately, and this was one of Hitler's two biggest blunders; the other one being his decision to attack Russia.

CHAPTER 2

The next main blunder of WWII was our **failure to provide convoys** to better protect our ships from German Subs at the beginning of the war. **They murdered our shipping**! The Brits knew how to do this, but it took us a while to catch on. And, unquestionably, there was the blunder of America **underestimating the Japanese, and the Germans.** Another recorded blunder in the history of the war was most certainly, President Franklin D. Roosevelt's comment where, in an impromptu speech, he said that he would demand "**unconditional surrender**" from Germany. Propaganda minister, Joseph Goebbels felt that FDR did them a favor which would, most likely, persuade the doomed Germans to fight to the last man, and that is exactly how they fought. Certainly, an American presidential blunder, but only a minor one. I was only nine years old when Pearl Harbor was bombed. As a kid, I was afraid that the Japanese were going to bomb us at home until I heard the encouragement that FDR always gave to the nation. Hell, because of him, I believed, after the first week of the war, that we were going to win the war. My sixth-grade teacher asked the class to write a poem of 60 words or less about the war. Here is what I wrote as a sixth grader, based on the President's repeated assurances:

> Our ships had holes as big as caves
> We couldn't bury our dead in graves
> We had the courage to fight on,
> although most of our men were gone.
> We'll fight the Germans to the last man
> And then we'll start on sneaky Japan
> And when we really start to fight
> The Japanese will die of fright.

Now, after the war ended, I was asked by my brothers when they came home from the war, how I knew back in 1941 that the Germans would be defeated before the Japanese, and why I referred to the Japanese as "sneaky". I told them that in my mind, Japan was a million miles away while I felt that England, being close to Germany, would help us defeat them way before we defeated Japan. I didn't know why I knew that, and that it was just something I felt, and that I called them sneaky because while they were in Washington talking peace, they were bombing us at Pearl Harbor. I got a pat on the head for that answer. During the war years, I fondly remember that when class began, we all stood up proudly, placed our hands over our hearts and recited the Pledge of Allegiance, after which, the teacher led us in a prayer to keep our soldiers safe. Yes sir, we were taught patriotism in those days, and were proud little Americans. Today, they have taken all that out of the schools. How sad! It has become the initial steps in the demise of America. But I am confident it will never come to pass. At a minimum, I want to see Patriotism back in the classrooms.

Now let's take a little stroll down the lane to none other than, **General Lucas at Anzio**, who was cautiously complaining that supplies were not commensurate with the expected high goals of that campaign. He, therefore, was **acting like a responsible officer**. Even though he was right, **he was accused of wasting precious time digging in and holding fast,** allowing the Germans precious time to regroup.

Patton, on the other hand, was a reckless forge ahead general. For the most part, Patton's blunders were usually swept under the rug because America needed a two-pistol packing General Hero in Europe. But, Patton was an embarrassment to Eisenhower **most of the time**! Had an enlisted man **slapped Patton**, he would have gone before a firing squad for this wartime offense. All Patton had to do was make a "**Half-Ass Apology**" for the slap. What a joke! This is **another classic example of RHIP's disgusting abuse**. This is also another classic example of why Generals felt that they were untouchable for any wrongdoings, and, this is why enlisted men were awakened to the fact that **rules did not apply to officers**.

Back to Patton, he was **psychotic,** suffering from grandeurs of self, with delusions and hallucinations, as he easily escaped from reality. He believed he had been on the battlefields with the Corinthians. God, he loved the war, and he loved himself even more! His **mental instability** was the very core of his aggressive military battle style, which helped him become one of our highly-decorated heroes of the war. Wars have always needed heroes to decorate. He certainly wound up being one of those prima donnas. In the movie, 'PATTON', an Army Chaplain said to Patton, "I noticed that you have a Bible by your bed. Do you read it often?" In the movie, his answer was, "<u>Every God Damn Day</u>"! Whether this was Hollywood or actual, is yet to be determined. His demeanor, however, fits the answer the movie provided.

CHAPTER 3

Let me admit that it is relatively easy for me to armchair quarterback most of these events, and that is exactly what I have done. Damn, if I was that smart, I could have given our leaders all the necessary advice to end the war in two weeks. However, I have reported facts and nothing else, so, as the reader, you must do with these facts as you will.

It was now 1951, and I had just graduated from high school and married my high school sweetheart three days later; no, she was not pregnant. I was living in Sarasota, Florida, at the time, and went on up to my brother's home in New Jersey to live, while waiting to see if the Army was going to draft me; since the Korean War was in full force. After about eight months in Jersey, the Florida draft board notified my sister in Sarasota, Florida, that I was supposed to have reported to the draft board three months ago. When she gave me the bad news, I decided that I would rather go into the Air Force so I could fly everywhere, rather than walk. So, back to Florida, we drove, and after proving that my wife was not pregnant, I was permitted to join the Air Force, where I stayed for 27 plus years; the greatest decision of my entire life.

After twelve weeks of brutal basic training at hot, muggy, San Antonio, Texas, during June, July, and August; which could have been accomplished in about six weeks, I was sent to Radio

Operator School at Keesler Air Force Base, in Biloxi, Mississippi. The first thing I saw when I got off the train, and walked toward the military bus, was a sign on the lawn of a house that read, "<u>Airmen and Dogs Keep Off The Grass</u>"! Wow; what a wonderful welcome. I was later informed when I reported to the base that folks from Biloxi were not happy with the military infiltrating their precious town of Biloxi, even though the base employed 16,000 Biloxi civilians. This was hard for me to comprehend since most Biloxi citizens worked on the base, and the military payroll, which was staggering, brought thousands of dollars into their economy every month.

Radio Operator School lasted a total of one year. The training was very extensive as we were taught how to send and receive Morse Code at a high speed of 20 words a minute. In addition, they taught us how to take care of minor breakdowns of our transmitters and receivers, and something that was called a Beat Frequency Oscillator, which allowed us to seek and find frequencies where the enemy might be transmitting. We also were trained to use the typewriter as we heard the code, and we learned how to read weather maps. We also had the opportunity to fly in the B-25 Billy Mitchell Bomber to learn airborne radio operating.

All of this was like being in a movie for this kid from Hoboken, New Jersey. From what we were told, our training cost in the neighborhood of $125,000; a pretty expensive neighborhood for 1952. I graduated at the very top of my class, and was offered a third stripe as a Buck Sergeant, and a job as an instructor at the school, which I took. After four years as an instructor, I was notified that I was being shipped to Japan, but not as a Radio Operator, as the Radio Operator field had become surplus with twice as many operators that were needed. When I asked why, after all my training, I would no longer be a radio operator, they told me that this cut was affecting over 2500 operators because we trained too many. I had the option at this point to get out of the service since my four-year hitch was up or reenlist for six years. I reenlisted for six and received a thousand dollars for each year giving me a $6,000 signing bonus, and a promotion to Staff Sergeant. Sounded like a good deal to me. After four years in Biloxi, I found that the people of the town were not hostile like that sign portrayed that I saw when I first arrived at Biloxi. I went to church in town and met some nice people. I truly loved Biloxi, as it was the best fishing spot on the planet with the Gulf at our doorstep and hundreds of inland waterways. In the military, we had a saying. **"Don't get to like the place where you are stationed because if you do, you will be shipped out sooner than you had hoped"**. Throughout my 27-year career, I found that to be very true.

After spending $125,000 on my Radio Operator training, and then having me instruct **too many** radio operators for four years, turned out to be one of the biggest **blunders** that directly affected me! But, sorry; this is just another of the many classic blunders I shall address in this book. Oh, oh, here it comes; "**UNCLE SAM; YOU'RE AN IDIOT!**" Well, at least I thought it was rather dumb to train me and 2500 others only to say "<u>Goodbye</u>."

So, off I went for the Japan tour of duty, not knowing what my job would be. When I arrived, I was told that because of my two years of college, I would be sent to the Legal Department, called The Staff Judge Advocate Office. There was no Legal Specialist School at the time. I had to burn the midnight oil, complete correspondence courses, and self-train myself, which I did successfully. This maneuver by the military, to ship me overseas, and have no clue as to why or where I was to be assigned, was another wake-up call for me. "<u>UNCLE SAM; YOU'RE STILL AN IDIOT</u>"!

During my four years in Japan, I was the chief military justice clerk. I was also a court reporter. I learned all aspects of the military legal field including the preparation of legal documents such as Wills, Power of Attorney, Separation agreements, and a variety of things for the purpose of rendering legal assistance to our troops. I also became proficient in handling claims for and against the government. Our young lawyers were right out of law school and didn't know shit from Shinola, as the saying goes. They relied heavily upon the NCOs with experience in the legal field. I was quite satisfied with what I had taught myself, as was my boss, the Staff Judge Advocate, Colonel Maurice Biddle. He was perhaps the greatest Officer and military lawyer I had ever come across. Definitely one of the very best!

I might add that I was quite surprised by the courtesies of the Japanese people. It became difficult to accept that they were once our bitter enemy. I spent a lot of time studying the Japanese language and Japanese customs. I noticed particularly, how the school children were so very orderly and well behaved unlike the hooligans in the U.S. My studies with the language opened many avenues of joy for me and my family during my four-year tour. On many occasions, I was needed as an interpreter during contacts with Japanese attorneys. It was one of my most memorable tours of duty during my 27-year career.

There was an occasion where a serviceman was driving his car in downtown Fukuoka and while making a left turn and crossing a railroad crossing, he had to stop on the tracks due to stopped vehicles in front and in back of him. The street car operator saw his car stopped but proceeded slowly until he hit the car in the right side damaging two doors in the shape of the front of the street car. He was smiling like a kamikaze pilot just before impact. To make a long story short, because of my ability to converse in Japanese, the Japanese allowed me to represent the soldier's claim against the street car company, even though I was not a lawyer.

The court informed me that the street car tracks were a sacred domain, and the street car always has the right of the tracks to proceed in a straight line regardless of any obstruction, telling me it was written law. I asked,

"Does that mean that a woman holding a baby on these sacred tracks would be run over?" This seemed to throw a wrench in their statement of their sacred domain to which they said, "No, that would be a different thing." I then came back with,

"Then the tracks are not that sacred, are they?" Again, confusion erupted causing the judge and their defending attorney to have their own side bar conference. I asked why the claimant's representative was not invited to the side bar discussion as is the case in the United States? I was told, "This is not the United States!" I said, in English, "Thank God", to which I was questioned to repeat what I said, in Japanese. My answer was, "I was having my own side bar conference to which you cannot have privy". This confused them enough to dismiss any further questions as to my stupid remarks. The Judge then looked at me in a strange way with a smile on his face and asked, "Do you have any information for this court which will cause us to disregard our law of the tracks having domain?" I said, "Yes sir. I would like to explain a concept we use in the United States."

The judge interrupted me and said,

"We are not interested in American law and you can't use it in this court." I replied, "Great your honor, because this is not American law that I shall be referring to, it is a doctrine. I don't know a word in Japanese for doctrine, but simply put, it is merely an acceptable belief of people using logic and reasoning to solve a problem when all else fails. May I proceed?" The Judge nodded his head and looked over to the court's lawyer as if to indicate, his lack of interest. I said, "Sir, in America there is a doctrine as concerns accidents with vehicles. It is called The Doctrine of Last Clear Chance, and it is not a law. And simply put, it states whichever person in an accident has the last clear chance to avoid that accident, then that person must avoid the accident. I therefore submit that the claimant was totally stopped on these sacred tracks and was blocked by vehicles, but the streetcar operator kept coming until he hit the claimant, smiling while he did it. Now since you indicated that the woman with the baby was an excusable situation allowing this court to <u>disregard their own law of domain on the tracks,</u> then why can't this court use the wisdom and logic of The Doctrine of Last Clear Chance, not as a law from my country, but as a more than reasonable solution to this problem? If you would not run over a woman with a baby, then you should not condone a streetcar running into a man while sitting in his car waiting for traffic to clear. I beg your honor for a fair ruling in favor of the claimant."

After a brief recess of about 10 minutes, the court was called to order. The Judge then said, "Sergeant, I am most interested in hearing more about the Doctrine you used as the claimant's defense and would like to discuss it with you after we are through if that is fine with you," I said, "I would be honored to spend the time with you and will also mail you complete information on this doctrine." The Judge looked over at my client, then looked to the court's lawyer and said, "I rule that the streetcar company will pay reasonable damage for the car of the claimant upon receipt of a reasonable repair bill. Judgment is for the Claimant and these proceedings are closed."

Wow, I was flabbergasted! So was the young soldier. The Court's lawyer congratulated me, but in the true Japanese tradition, he lost face as the Judge later told me, since he was beaten by a non-lawyer. I invited the court's lawyer to my base at Itazuke Air Base in Kasugabaru only 5 miles from the town of Fukuoka where I introduced him to Colonel Biddle and the other young lawyers we had. We later formed a Japanese/American Lawyers guild which met once a month to discuss crimes and offenses between the Japanese and the Americans. It was a great system causing better understanding of each other's problems. I was very proud of that accomplishment and gained a greater respect for the Japanese. Colonel Biddle said, "Sarge, you're amazing!"

After my four years in Japan, and upon returning to the good old U.S.A. in 1959, I was happy to be assigned to Orlando AFB, Florida, since I called Florida my home, and my sister was now living there, having moved from Sarasota. Colonel Biddle pulled some strings to get me the assignment. I was there for only one year when I was notified that I was going to be sent to Iceland for a year. The Navy oversaw Keflavik Naval Air Base, and the Air Force only had one Air Force Captain who needed a legal specialist as we had Air Force troops as well as Navy and Marine troops at the base. Our boss at the legal office was a naval captain which is the same as our full Colonel. Believe it or not his name was, Captain Robert E. Lee. He was a fine officer who had the troop's interests at heart. I was privileged to have served under this officer. My tour in Iceland was uneventful with six months of daytime, six months of nighttime, and the Aurora Borealis ever flashing during the night cycle. Upon my return to the United States, I was assigned to Strategic Air Command's,

Westover Air Force Base, in Springfield, Massachusetts. Shortly after my arrival, my wife developed incurable cancer. Since the prognosis was terminal, I was allowed to transfer back to Orlando since I needed my sister to help with my two young sons, Rob and Steve of nine and seven years old. This transfer was called a "Compassionate Transfer" and would be good for only two years, after which, you needed to be available for assignments, or get out of the service. My wife of eleven years passed away at the age of 28, and I found myself living at my sister's house with my two sons. This was not a great time in my life, but within a year or so, I met and married my second wife to whom I have been married to for over 56 years, at this point in the writing of this book. I guess you could say it worked.

After three years, it was now time for me to leave Orlando, Florida because Vietnam was waiting for me and the Air Force could not continue that war without me! The next blunder came when we were to receive combat training before going into combat. I was sent to the rifle firing range to re-qualify with the rifle, even though I was a qualified Sharp Shooter. Well, the rifle was an old M-1 Carbine, but in the Nam, they were using M-16s. The shooting range Sergeant told me that, "a rifle was a rifle". I had to ask him if that were true, then why the hell they even invented the M-16; to which I got no response. Oh, oh, here it comes again: "THANKS UNCLE SAM FOR NOT HAVING THE AUTHORIZED COMBAT RIFLE FOR ME TO FAMILIARIZE WITH, SO THAT I WOULD BE COMBAT READY"!

I would be going to Vietnam in a month. It was now early June of 1968, and the thought of leaving was very uncomfortable to me. The war was in full blast and it was a period when not too many active-duty people were looking forward to the type of war they would be supporting. Yes, <u>TYPE OF WAR</u>, which requires explanation, and which I shall provide later. The thought of leaving my two young sons, and my two-year old daughter Lisa, was a rather depressing thought for not only me, but for them as well. When I received a tape from my wife shortly after my arrival in Vietnam, and heard my two-year old try to say, "Hi Daddy", while she stuttered profusely; I was shocked! We were extremely close, and my wife explained that her stuttering started a few days after I left the country. This was not a happy event for me to have on my mind, but I'm sure all of the GI's had a burden or two to carry with them into combat.

Other than knowing that I was on my way to Vietnam, I had no clue as to where I was going to be in country. Upon my arrival in Vietnam, I was on my way to where I was told our headquarters building was located, when a siren began to wail. Never having heard an air raid siren before, except when watching a film on London being bombed, I didn't know what my next step was going to be, so I began running. I was looking for a direction to run, but people were running in all different directions! I finally just picked up the closest bunch and ran with them. I discovered that they were all trying to get into what they called <u>a bunker</u>. <u>What a joke!</u> The <u>military provided no bunkers</u> so, the men built their own, which they thought were safe enough, but which were, in fact, <u>death traps</u>! They dug a trench about six feet down and inside was an area cut out about 12'X16'. On the inside walls, they placed sandbags; why, I have no idea, because they were already six feet down! Then they had about four rows of sandbags around the top perimeter, and on top of them, they used the world war two metal pieces that were fitted together to make the runway strips. The British who invented the stuff, called these steel plates, Marston Mats; we called them PSP. It was always the Navy Seabees who built the PSP Air Strips. On top of the PSP metal strips were a hundred or more sandbags scattered all over the place. In order to get in the bunker fast, you had to duck your head down just as you were running in and entering, or you would run into the side of the metal mat, which I did, as I was trying to duck and get in, but was pushed before I could duck. Here go another one of my negatives, "**Thank you Uncle Sam for the Bunkers you didn't provide!**" This is crazy, first no combat M-16 Rifle for combat familiarization, and now no friggin bunker for safety from combat hostility. How the hell ready were we for this war? Shit, the U.S. was already there about 10 years but was floundering like they didn't have a clue as to why we were there! This is still impossible to comprehend when I look back on these events. As time went on during my tour, I began to wonder what the hell kind of a combat zone this was, and why everyone didn't seem to give a shit. After a few enemy, rockets flew over onto the airstrip about 100 yards behind us, and within about five minutes, the siren then gave an all-clear. I proceeded over to the orderly room, (I don't know why we called headquarters the orderly room, because it was never very orderly) and I reported in. I noticed the minute I got off the plane that **the air smelled**

<u>like warm rancid rusty water</u>, which was the odor of a spray on the foliage called <u>Agent Orange</u>, a substance we used to clear jungle mass so as to have a better view of the enemy's advances. It also gave them a better view of us; <u>wasn't that brilliant?</u> The humidity contained this awful smell constantly and you never got used to it. After my retirement from the service, I learned that Agent Orange was proven to be the cause of Prostate Cancer and Type II Diabetes, which I now had both, years later.

I had my stateside fatigues which were not conducive to the climate of Vietnam as they were of heavy material. I asked where I could get my combat boots and my combat thin weight fatigues. The asshole at the desk said,

"Downtown Saigon, where else?"

Hell, I didn't even know where Saigon was, nor had I ever heard of the place. I thought he was trying to be funny but discovered that he wasn't. He said that a supply warehouse was raided a month ago, and everything was stolen. He then said,

"If you want fucking combat clothing, they are available on the black-market downtown in Saigon, as I told you."

I then said, sarcastically, "Is that where I will get my M-16 rifle that I don't know how to shoot, to fight the bastards who raided the supply warehouse?" He answered,

"No", with a smirk on his face. We keep them locked in a metal conex container outside, and when you need a rifle, it will be disbursed by a Sergeant who is in charge of the storage conex; good luck on that, however!

I then was forced to have some dialog with this young one striper who didn't seem to be impressed by the five stripes I was wearing. I started with,

"Airman; I need you to get the hell out of your chair, look me in the fucking eye, and answer my questions like you give a shit!

I guess he had been getting away with acting like an asshole since this seemed to later be the attitude of just about everybody in Vietnam. **Discipline was practically non-existent**. Being my first trip to a combat zone, it looked like it was going to be just like it was always negatively portrayed in World War II movies. He got up and immediately said,

"I'm sorry Sergeant. I'm having a bad day, and these fucking air raids scare the living shit out of me. It takes me a while to settle back down." I then said,

"What base is this, and do we have a lot of air raids?" He replied,

"This is Bien Hoa. We are an ammo dump and they knock the shit out of us every fucking night."

I was able to detect immediately from the demeanor of this young man, that he was scared, frustrated, and totally out of his element. I asked him where I was to bunk and where I could get my bedding. He walked to a closet behind him and gave me two sheets, a pillow and pillowcase, and one blanket. He then said, "I'll show you your quarters Sarge."

A few doors down were rows of barracks that had no walls. Well, the walls were just louvers from the ground to the roof with a screen behind them. The louvers kept the rain out, and let the air in. The private then said, "We call these Huts, or Hooches, but not barracks. You will have to be the Hut Chief since you will be the ranking man of the other eleven guys." I then asked, "What does a Hut Chief do?" His answer was,

"Any fucking thing he wants to." I then said,

"You're being an asshole again!" To which he replied,

"There are no duties, you're just their boss."

After making my bed and feeling kind of hungry, I found out where the chow hall was and proceeded there to eat. The food was good and plentiful. One great thing was, the cook would ask how many steaks you wanted before he would ask how you wanted them cooked. I figured from this point on, if I was killed in the NAM, at least I would die on a full stomach.

As hot as it was with 98 degree temperatures day or night and humidity just as high all year long, it was surprisingly a cool feeling at night as these louvered huts seemed to magnify any of the breezes from outside. It felt like your sheets were wet, which kind of gave a false feeling that it was cool and comfortable.

The next day, I was to report to my duty section which was the Base Staff Judge Advocate Office. I was what civilians call, a Paralegal. In the military, we called it a Legal Specialist. There was a Sergeant whose rank was equal to mine, but he had more time in that grade and was supposed to be what is known as the NCOIC, which stands for Non-Commissioned Officer in Charge. After meeting my boss, a Major, he welcomed me and said that he got notification that I was needed as NCOIC at Tan Son Nhut Air Base in Saigon, and that they wanted me there today. I was pleased after hearing this because this would be my first opportunity of being in charge of the enlisted men and, for the first time in my career, being the NCOIC; a necessary credential for advancement and to continue leading lower ranking men. So, after unplugging and saying goodbye to the private in the orderly room who handed me my orders for my new assignment, I was given a driver and a Jeep to head on into Saigon, which was southwest of Bien Hoa. It was a dirt road trip that took about two hours. It was kind of creepy because you were always waiting for something to happen. Fortunately, nothing happened. After my arrival, and getting situated with quarters, I reported to my duty section. My new boss, a Major, informed me that he had three young Airman who was kind of out of hand, and a Tech Sergeant who was no help at all. These Airmen were not actually Legal Specialists, nor was the Tech Sergeant, but all four were from different jobs being used as fill ins. I immediately understood their apparent lack of interest. It was the same attitude I saw from the clerk in Bien Hoa. I told my boss that I would take them into the courtroom and would try to get something accomplished. He said,

"Sarge, you do whatever you think is necessary. You will have my full backing. Just see if you can either get them going, or get them the hell out of here; they're useless."

I then called the men into the courtroom and began my meeting in the following manner, to the best of my memory.

"Guys, I'm Technical Sergeant Berry. I am a Legal Specialist. I am here to perform a miracle, and you will be my little miracles." With this comment, I noticed them looking at each other and smirking like a bunch of high school kids. I then went on to say,

"Let's face it guys, you and I are not going to win this fucking war in Vietnam by being Legal Specialists, but let me try to tell you why you are here. Better yet, let's go around the room and have each of you tell me why you think you are here." Going to each one at a time, here is kind of what I got from the first young man,

"Sarge, I'm here because I joined the Air Force to stay out of the Army and Vietnam, and I find myself in Vietnam anyhow, so I'm kind of pissed. Since I'm here, what the hell can I do, I don't even have a rifle because they don't let the Air Force guys carry one around on the base like the Army guys? Some of these Army guys are just kids even younger than me, but I am not trusted enough to have my own rifle? Kind of knocks the wind out of my sail. I never heard of a military fighting man in a combat zone without having a fucking rifle. I don't like feeling like a nobody piece of shit! So, my morale is in the toilet. And I have a continuous uneasy feeling by not being combat ready with a rifle. There are other things that bother me also, but you probably don't want to hear them." Hearing this, I then said,

"You know what; after work tonight, you guys are all going to the NCO Club with me and the Sarge here, so we can relax and get to know each other, then we can all share our problems. I want you to hear mine also, OK?"

Surprisingly, they smiled and seemed to like the idea. I went in and told the Major what had transpired, and he said, "Hey, it's only an hour away from quitting time, go ahead and take them now."

The NCO Club was just around the corner and off we went. I had to get special permission to let three enlisted men who were not NCOs come in with me. Basically, and to make a long story short, I told them that their morale was down because they were not trained Legal Specialists and felt out of place trying to work in the job, and that it was certainly understandable. I explained that I entered the legal field the same way. I promised them I would have an M-16 Rifle and a 45 pistol with plenty of ammo for each of them within a few days, while not even having a clue as to how I was going to do this. What pissed me off was that every friggin Air Force officer in the NAM wore a 45 on his side, like a drugstore cowboy, but the NCOs and lower rank enlisted could not have a weapon. I know, I'm picking on officers again. Now, what kind of shit was that? I also informed them that I would give each of them a specific job and train them in the required skills. I told them I would teach them all how to prepare a Will, a Power of Attorney, military justice basics, and how to use a steno-mask and be a court reporter for our courts-martial's. Finally, I promised that I would go as far as possible to get them each another stripe for a sincere effort on their part. They were kind of sold, but perhaps not sure I could deliver. The real problem, I discovered, was that they had no lower ranking Legal Specialists in Vietnam and these guys came from other fields to fill in a job that was totally mind-boggling to them. This is the same way in which I was introduced to the legal field. So, it was my job to make them all Legal Specialists. I looked forward to the challenge, and if I may brag, became very proud of them within a relatively short period.

Then, out of the clear blue sky, I discovered that the gun Sergeant who had the key to open the conex to distribute rifles if we were under attack, was living in the Hut that I was going to be the Hut Chief. Remembering what the clerk in Bien Hoa told me, that I could do anything I wanted, I took the Sergeant to the gun storage container called a conex, and he was confused as to what I was up to. I said, "Sarge, I'm a Legal Specialist at the Judge Advocate's Office. If you ever get into a jam, I will be there for you; trust me, you'll need me. Here is what you can do for me in the meantime. I need four M-16s, and four 45 pistols with holsters and boxes of ammo for them. I see you have oodles of them in here. Here is why I need them. My Major, who is the Judge Advocate of the base, has the responsibility of making what's called solatium payments to Vietnamese families who have been hurt or killed as a result of our combat activities. This special mission is very dangerous. Sometimes he must take one to three of us in a Jeep to dangerous villages to transact this business. He needs and wants us armed, and the military police are not available to render that service. When local Vietnamese are hurt or family members killed because of our military combat activities, we must go down in dangerous areas and give them a stack of money that, in their culture, shows remorse for their loss. Payment of this form, in their culture, is an apology in the way of a condolence payment. Now, if you refuse me, I'll have to go to the Base Commander who, I'm sure, will give us what we need. What do you say?" He immediately replied without hesitation, "Sergeant Berry, go get your Jeep, and I'll help you load it up." When I arrived at the Base Legal Office with all the weaponry, the guys were blown out of their friggin minds. It's funny how when I see the movie, 'From Here to Eternity', I remember where the base was under attack and the Sergeant with the key **wouldn't open the conex** without the Colonel's OK. That incident in the movie, although a Hollywood script, was so routinely true in the Air Force; I'm sad to say.

Well, now we moved a desk under an attic door and stood on it to place the guns and ammo in hiding where we could get it in a moment's notice. We preloaded the gun magazines. It wound up being a blessing in disguise two days later.

I was just sitting outside in the office Jeep next to the office making a voice tape to my wife when more than 300 Viet Cong had overrun the front gate that had only one guard. He was killed. This was the beginning of many such offenses that were called **"THE TET OFFENSIVES"**. Our office was not more than a football field away from the front gate. Hearing the firing of weapons and the siren blast, we got the guns and ammo down. As I stated, the guns were already pre-loaded. While other people were trying to find the Sarge with the key, we were able to lie in hiding and started shooting at these bastards running in the street towards us, which delayed them long enough for somebody to find the Sarge, get the key, and about 50 of our guys now being able to shoot at them. Every damn one of those bastards was killed. We got no medals for this; hell, we were soldiers and what we did was expected! Bull shit! Had we not had the loaded guns available, we all would have been targets! Did we get any recognition for this? Hell no! Instead, the Squadron Commander asked how we got our guns so fast. Another ass hole. Most of the dead VC (Viet Cong), after looking, were just young kids. Not a nice scene. Did I become a hero with my guys after that? What do you think? Funny thing, my wife would record a tape and send it to me, then I would record over it and send it to her. Since I was outside sitting in the Jeep recording just before the commotion at the front gate, and the recorder was still running when I abruptly ran into the building to get weapons, I later assumed that the end of the tape was where I finished my recording. So, I mailed the tape back to my wife who heard a lot of shouting and yelling on the tape which I didn't know was on the tape. This didn't go over too well with her, since I told her we were far from actual combat areas. Well, it was only a little white lie. I don't believe we really knew how our families must have felt hearing of the daily casualties in Vietnam and fearing for our lives. The military should have given them medals.

The heavy bombing had taken place several days before in an unsafe area of Saigon called Cholon. This city was notorious for hoodlums, Viet Cong hides a-ways and just a bad place in general. Certainly, not the kind of place you would want to take your girlfriend! Nevertheless, the Solatium payment had to be given to the family. The Major was going down by himself because nobody wanted to go to Cholon; any place but there! Why he didn't tell them to get their ass in the Jeep remains a mystery to me. I told him I would drive and he could ride shotgun with the M-16. He was pleased with the idea, and off we went. One of his younger Captains told me on the QT that the Major was uneasy about leaving the base without me.

When we got to Cholon, we were being looked at as if we were shark bate. Very creepy-looking people seemed ready to pounce on us. My sitting in the Jeep with the M-16 held kind of high was a very good deterrent; apparently. The Major went on into the shack after being invited as they knew that a nice stack of money with a red ribbon tied around it was in his briefcase. When he started to come out of the shack, shooting erupted from all different directions. He hit the ground and yelled at me to take off. To my immediate right, about three feet away was a ditch wide as about two widths of the Jeep, and about five feet deep. The Jeep was running and I laid the M-16 on the floor of the jeep between the two front seats and quickly pulled into the ditch. I took my weapon and crawled to the edge of the ditch where I could see the Major pinned down. He saw me and said, "I told you to get the hell out of here, I don't have a damn chance!" Trying to lighten the situation I then yelled, and I don't know why, "<u>Fuck you Major; I'm going to get you out!</u> I'll start shooting at the directions where the fire is coming from so you can get your ass into this fucking ditch just like in the movies, let's go!" While the writing of this sounds like I was cool, calm and collected, I could actually hear and feel my heart beating, but I didn't shit in my pants; well, almost didn't.

I began a barrage with my automatic M-16 (the one I was not trained how to shoot), as the Major was able to get up and run, then roll into the ditch. As he did that, I threw him the M-16, and got into the driver's side of the Jeep while he jumped into the other side. We sped down the ditch for about 50 yards, and as the ditch was coming to an end, I got back up to the dirt road as we kept going as fast as we could. Two bullets came from behind us to the right of my head and through the windshield, and to the left of the Major's head and through the windshield. Long story short, we got back, and on into Tan Son Nhut Air Base.

I guess that my best combat training came from war movies; especially the John Wayne movies. The Major asked me to drive to the front of the Base Commander's office and wait for him. The Base Commander came out to look at the holes in the windshield. I remember him saying, "Holy Shit, you guys almost bought the farm!" I remember getting a smile from the Commander when I said, "They wouldn't sell us the farm sir."

I slept like a baby that night. What the saying means when you say you slept like a baby in Vietnam is, that "you cried all night and shit in your pants." Oh, oh, here comes the negative;

"THANK YOU UNCLE SAM FOR THE ARMORE PLATED VEHICLE YOU DIDN'T PROVIDE FOR A FUCKING MISSION THAT NEEDED ONE, AND AN ARMED SECURITY POLICE ESCORT THAT IS NEVER AVAILABLE!"

When the Major told the three Captains, and the enlisted men in the office what happened, they looked over at me and said, "Wooo, Audie Murphy"! From then on, they jokingly called me Sergeant Audie. That evening, just as the 5 o'clock quitting time came up, beer cans were popping open, as every office in Vietnam drank a beer at that time. The guys in the office gathered and held their cans toward me and one of the officers said, "Sarge, you are one in a million; kind of a crazy bastard, and we are so glad you came to Tan Son Nhut." This was like Audie Murphy receiving the Congressional Medal of Honor. It was a great feeling. I now had respect and rapport with the egg head enlisted guys who were not seen as egg heads anymore as they were training well, and the young officers were amazed at what I had done for the Major. This was perhaps one of my greatest accomplishments of that friggin war. Back to the popping of the beer cans. For your tour in Vietnam, you did not drink water. When we boiled water and ran it through a funnel with cotton stuffed in it, the water was still a light yellow in color and had some kind of movement of swirling things. So, we used water to shower and to flush a toilet, but drank beer to keep from getting sick. In the chow hall, we drank powdered milk and black coffee, but I'm sure they used water to prepare them. Yuk! There was no such thing as water bottles in those days.

A week passed and the Major said, the Base Commander wanted to see us in his office. I figured, oh boy, another lovely mission. When we got over there, all the enlisted, officers from our office were standing by smiling. The Commander told me that for my extraordinary bravery in the line of duty, and with disregard for my own safety, thereby rescuing the Major from almost sudden death, I was being awarded the Bronze Star. Everyone applauded and congratulated me. I said,

"Colonel, thank you for this award, but I certainly hope the Major, who was pinned down under heavy enemy fire, receives a similar award." He assured me that such an award was already in progress.

Damn! I now felt like I needed to celebrate not only the event but the fact that I was alive to celebrate. I had to go to the NCO CLUB and get drunk with my friends to do this, but this didn't happen. As we were all leaving the Commander's office, the air raid siren went off. I never ran to the Bunkers anymore, and I got to where I just stayed in the office which I felt was much safer because it had concrete walls. The office was just across the street. Several guys were killed on a hit from a rocket in those makeshift bunkers I described earlier. My motto was if you saw a red round circle coming in, run like hell and hit the deck, but if you saw a red streak across the sky, it wasn't coming your way.

Vietnam had a way of removing your common sense. One tended to do things without forethought and developed the attitude that, if their number was up, then it would be up. It became an, "I don't give a shit" attitude. I began to understand the attitude I observed at Bien Hoa as being a way of life in Vietnam. For me, it even got to the point where, if I was walking or riding my bike back from the chow hall, and if it started raining, I didn't run or pump my bike any faster. The rain felt good and cooled me off, and, I just didn't give a shit about getting wet, and it didn't just rain in Vietnam, it poured buckets at a time. It's not amazing to me that these men were coming back with PTSD because after a year or more of combat events, they developed a totally different mindset, and some were able to come back to the real world mentally, while some were not. Certainly, nothing to be ashamed of if you could not. The daily thoughts of whether you would become a fatality from one of the many rocket attacks, was truly scary. When you were awakened each night from the sound of the loud siren, the shrill of the siren went through you like a knife. The Viet Cong were great about making sure you never got a full night's sleep as they often hit the base with rockets at about three in the morning.

CHAPTER 4

During an evaluation at the VA about 12 years later, I was asked how many rocket attacks we had at Tan Son Nhut during my year there. I indicated that I counted them by cutting a notch on a square wooden post next to my bed. I had over 178 notches on that post during my 12- month tour. In a report that the evaluator prepared after our interview, when I received my copy, I was shocked by what he wrote. Here were his comments:

"This veteran stated that he recalled over 178 rocket attacks at his base in Vietnam. My research revealed that there were somewhere in the neighborhood of 22 rocket attacks."

This was the same evaluator who didn't know that my Bronze Star was a combat medal.

I later contested both his disbeliefs and my research revealed that he left a 3 off the 22 figure he reported. In essence, 223 attacks. 22 rocket attacks would have been a picnic. Rocket attacks were heavy at Tan Son Nhut because this is where all the planes that bombed the shit out of Hanoi daily were housed.

I found out by accident one evening, that in an open compound about the size of three tennis courts, we would have an outdoor movie three times a week, or whenever film was available. We would all sit on the ground, bring our snacks and try to enjoy 'The Good, The Bad, and The Ugly', with Clint

Eastwood. What I was not aware of was that, shortly after it became dark in the Nam, it usually began to down pour rain. It didn't bother the guys watching the movie because they brought their poncho rain coats with them, which they never issued me. This is one of the examples of the enjoyable things not provided us in this combat zone. The next day, trying to get a poncho, I was told; there were none. Oh, oh, here it comes: "<u>THANKS UNCLE SAM FOR NOT HAVING PONCHOS FOR EVERYBODY!</u>" "<u>GOD DAMN IT; IT RAINS EVERY DAMN DAY IN VIETNAM!</u>

Perhaps, at this point, we need to discuss some more of the Vietnam <u>Blunders,</u> which were, by no means, minor blunders. Here we had these <u>little brown badgers</u> living in tunnels which we could not find, and who came out whenever they desired to shoot us. They would cut a large bamboo into a half shell, which they used as a launching pad for their 122-mm rockets that they would launch with flashlight batteries! After the launch, when you sent fire into where the rocket launcher was, the VC was gone. These guys had over 100 years of practice while fighting the French, so to say that they were prepared for us would be an understatement.

Now here is the <u>Creme de la Creme!</u> We fought this war in the only way we knew how. We set up bases all through Vietnam at places like <u>Tan Son Nhut</u>, <u>Phu Cat</u>, <u>Da Nang</u>, <u>Bien Hoa,</u> <u>Phan Rang,</u> and <u>Cam Ran Bay,</u> to name a few. We built our <u>usual chain link fences</u> around these bases and called these fences, <u>THE PERIMETER</u>. I bet the word **perimeter** scared the shit out of enemy forces surrounding us. Now, this should keep you bastards out of our bases; we thought! Not only will you know exactly where we are, even though we don't know where the hell you are, but you will also be able to send in rockets to destroy our planes and kill our guys. Too bad we were not smart enough to keep our planes out in the bay on aircraft carriers as we do today. It took us over <u>TEN FUCKING YEARS</u> to figure that one out! Feel free to hit us you little bastards, because we will be ready for you; I think! We may have to ask for a time out though, because we will either be asleep, at the NCO Club getting drunk, the swimming pool, the photo hobby shop developing pictures, the recording department where we would be taping music, the leathercraft department, or we'll be looking for the Sergeant with the key to the Conex where the weapons are. Don't worry; we'll be ready! <u>NOT!</u>

<u>Come on Washington, come on Joint Chiefs of Staff, come on Mr. President</u>; this was the "<u>FUCKING TYPE OF WAR YOU WERE HAVING US FIGHT</u>?" General Westmoreland, didn't you even have a fucking clue? These damn combat zones throughout Vietnam were <u>GOD DAMN COUNTRY CLUBS</u>! Some Mamzy Pamzy Morale, Welfare, and Recreation Officer thought it would be good for our morale to have these luxuries in our sweet little combat zones. The only thing that helps a soldier's morale in a combat zone is to <u>defeat the fucking enemy</u>! <u>YOU CAN'T TURN A COMBAT ZONE INTO A MAMZY PAMZY SERVICE CLUB AND EXPECT THE MEN TO BE COMBAT READY</u>!; or am I missing the point? Why didn't somebody in Washington wake

up to smell the coffee? Didn't Westmoreland notice our country club atmosphere? Hell, we didn't have it this good at most stateside bases! No wonder when I was evaluated at the VA after my retirement, the evaluator didn't know that my Bronze Star was a combat medal! Surprisingly, US Air Force guys stationed at these bases throughout Vietnam <u>were not the real combat soldiers of that war</u>; I am not proud to state. It was the Army grunts and the Marines who were out in the boonies trying to fight a guerilla war that they were not properly trained or equipped to fight; contrary to popular belief. This is where the over 56,000 casualties occurred. There was no damn excuse for over 950 helicopters being shot down either, yet we kept sending them out into harm's way without a clue as to how to solve this problem. The Army grunts and the Marines were sent out in small patrols to find the enemy which they never did. The enemy was well entrenched in their underground tunnels which we were unable to find. They picked us off like a turkey shoot during these senseless missions. We just didn't have a handle on guerilla warfare.

<u>Get this!</u> The troops in the field received cases of Carlings Black Label Beer rather than water. They drank it as if it were water. Figure this one out! Also, the boys were growing marijuana out in the fields and under the hooches. What the hell were the leaders doing? Probably smoking the shit? I know this is all too difficult to believe, but <u>it damn sure was taking place</u>! Where the hell was our <u>academy graduates</u> when proper <u>planning to win</u> should have been <u>the only mandate?</u> Why did it only take me two days to figure out that

we were not combat ready at these bases? What was General Westmoreland doing besides making trips back to Washington and telling Secretary of Defense McNamara that things were going well, and that all he needed was another 100,000 troops? Supposedly, and by his own admission, Westmoreland had a free hand to run the war as he saw fit. He had, however, gone down in history as the General who lost the war in Vietnam, and rightfully so! He was a hell of a guy, an honest guy, but an ill equipped General. The problem with career officers is that they have this tremendous fear that if they make any radical decisions that backfire, it would tarnish their career. CAREER, CAREER, CAREER! Westmoreland didn't know what direction to go into. His advisors were just as dumb. To the Vietnamese, we were no longer a mighty military force they had heard about, but rather, a bunch of idiots who didn't know our ass from a hole in the ground! There was never any doubt in their minds that they would drive us out of their country, and that's exactly what they did to the forces in Vietnam who opposed their attempts to conquer the south. It makes me sick to think that we did not have a clue as to how to win this so-called war; not a damn clue! It was like trying to kill thousands of ants with a hammer if we knew where the ants were.

I hate to reveal the following combat tactic that must have been classified TOP SECRET, and I may have to go before a firing squad for revealing it, but, we had officers living in downtown Saigon in unbelievable Villas and Swank Hotels; living like rich men! They were not housed on the base! This is probably when the enemy realized that our hearts weren't really in it. Our officers loved Vietnam duty. It was a big picnic and they were having a ball.

In both the military and civilian sectors, there are always two kinds of people. The kind who do their jobs with pride to accomplish the mission, and the type who have no damn desire to do anything more than enhance their careers. If you want to know where our military blunders have always come from, I assure you they came from the career enhancement seekers! I'm ashamed to say that many of the officers I worked for were selfish, self-oriented, and pompous asses, with nothing more on their minds than enhancing their careers. It is my strong opinion that the entire officer corps, right on up to the academy graduates, need to throw out all its so-called <u>traditional bull shit</u>, and join modern times by <u>re-writing the officer's code of conduct</u>. How they act, and what they get away with is <u>beyond</u> description! Will there ever be a remedy for this problem?

<u>Never, never, because it will never be looked upon as a problem</u>! I have a brilliant idea. Let the NCOs write a new code for our officers. I don't think they would like what we write as their mandate to be <u>"an officer and a gentleman."</u> Obviously, it must appear, again, that I hate commissioned officers. Let me reiterate that it is only the officers who have lost their way in terms of what is needed and expected from them, that I detest. Certainly, there were good officers in the military, but not enough of them, but I certainly honored the good ones.

Yes, the blunders of Vietnam were almost too many to discuss, but I shall address the <u>**biggest blunder**</u> of that war. That blunder was the use of a chemical called, <u>AGENT ORANGE</u>. The ramifications of our veteran's exposure to this chemical were denied by our government at first, but they later admitted they were wrong. Even though the U.S. Government has thus far paid out $45 million in disability benefits to veterans, the real cost was the ailments it provided, not only to the veterans who were exposed but the offspring of their children who were born with debilitating birth defects. How toxic is this chemical? It has been determined that exposure to this herbicide can directly cause, Parkinson's Disease, Prostate Cancer, Respiratory cancers of the lung, larynx, trachea, and bronchus, Hodgkins Disease, non-Hodgkin's Lymphoma, Leukemia, Type 2 Diabetes, and Ischemic Heart Disease. At the writing of this book (2016), I have suffered from this exposure by experiencing Prostate Cancer (Prostate having had to be removed causing a multitude of debilitating health conditions such as impotency, incontinence, and erectile dysfunction, and Type 2 Diabetes (causing neuropathy of the legs, and numbness of the toes), and Respiratory lung problems known as COPD.

This chemical was used for the purpose of removing heavy foliage areas in order to preclude the enemy from hiding in heavy foliage. The chemical was produced by Monsanto Chemical Company, who has, thus far, avoided accountability for this dangerous substance. The Vietnamese Red Cross has revealed that nearly one million Vietnamese civilians including generations of children have been born with debilitating birth defects. At present, the U.S. Government has made no reparations for the Vietnamese. It was also determined that Airmen who had never been to Vietnam but who worked on aircraft from that war were exposed to contaminated aircraft that contained Agent Orange. This chemical lingers on everything it comes in contact with, by either breathing it, or by touching it, you become infected. Now, who was the person responsible for ordering that the shit be sprayed? **It was a Navy Admiral.** Rear Admiral Elmo Zumwalt, the commander of U.S. Naval Forces in Southeast Asia was the culprit who ordered the spraying of the defoliant over the South Vietnamese countryside to deprive Communist Troops of cover. Now why a Naval Admiral made that decision, rather than a land-based General, is puzzling to me. But here again, Admirals, Generals; they all do the same dumb things, once again proving that their power was so vast that they had no clue as to how to use that power. The U.S. Government endorsed the purchase of the shit, so this Admiral doesn't stand alone for ordering the spraying of the chemical. What a Circus!

CHAPTER 5

Now let's take a look at something called, "Rank Has Its Privileges". This concept continues to be abused by officers. It's also known commonly as RHIP. So, where is the proper delineation of where privileges should start and where they should end? Does this mean that if the Officer's mess hall is serving steak three times a week, then it would be proper for the Enlisted mess to have only hamburger as often instead? Does it mean that enlisted men should live in screened louvered Hootches in a combat zone, while officers live in air-conditioned swank hotels and Villas downtown? Is this what we mean by RHIP? You won't actually find any rules or laws that define this concept because it is nothing more than a long-standing ABUSED tradition that continues to be abused. I believe that officers think that enlisted men are too stupid to know the difference. That's what has happened yesterday, is happening today, and will happen tomorrow! Let's not kid ourselves! Career officers expect these privileges because that is what is instilled in their minds. Anything less would insult most officer's dignity. Some of the Officers I have worked with during my career felt that it was their duty to take care of the men under them, while most had no such desire. I had the highest respect for those officers who were mission-oriented, rather than self-oriented. Let me reveal a long-standing feeling of a large number of the enlisted men that I was associated with during my 27 years of service. The sad fact is; that <u>most enlisted men hate officers</u>! Yes, downright <u>hate them</u>! Some officers want you to salute them to satisfy their ego, while others want you to salute the insignia, and what it represents; as it should be at all times. In Vietnam, it was fairly common to find that a killed-in-action officer had a bullet wound in the back of the head. How do I know this? Our office was next door to the morgue. I visited the morgue daily when picking up my buddy who was assigned there, so we could go to the mess hall together. One day I asked him if he thought it was kind of strange that all the killed in action enlisted were shot from the front, and that an alarming number of officers had head wounds from the back. His fucking answer was,

"In Vietnam, everyone gets what they deserve! Make your own conclusion." At stateside bases, the best example of inequality that has always bothered me was how we didn't take care of our very young married with children enlisted men, <u>and still do not today!</u> While Officers and high-ranking Sergeants can live on base in very nice quarters, pay no rent, and pay no utilities, while merely forfeiting their <u>measly quarters' allowance</u>, a lower ranking enlisted man is rarely allowed to live on base, unless there is an over-abundance of living quarters, which there usually is not. Quarters Allowance for living off base provides about less than half the required rent, not inclusive of utilities. Yes, this is an <u>RHIP</u> thing that <u>needs to be scrapped!</u> Will it ever be equitable? I can assure you that <u>it will never be</u>; not in our lifetime! A young Airman under these circumstances usually finds a part-time job off base after work and weekends, while his wife does the same unless she must stay home with children. They usually QUALIFY FOR FOOD STAMPS, and this is an embarrassment to me and every young enlisted man in any of the branches of the military and should be to Congress. Having young enlisted men in our services living on the POVERTY LINE is downright embarrassing, disgusting, and unnecessary. Hey, these are guys and gals who are available to die for their country at a moment's notice! We need to channel all the money we waste in the military into a direction that would benefit those who have virtually no benefits, other than a paycheck that they can't live on. This unfortunate military personnel must work a part-time job, in addition to the 50-hour workweek they usually must work, which precludes them from bettering their military skills through study. It's a double-edge sword. This is another area where the taxpaying American has absolutely no knowledge. Congress rarely addresses this issue as they are preoccupied in passing legislation that raises their own pay and increases their benefits. On numerous occasions during my service, even after the Government Accounting Office (GOA) provided surveys that showed that the enlisted man was living on the poverty line, Congress would get two raises in a row before they would approve one for us. Our raises were always too late to catch up with the cost of living. To this issue I must say, HEY; IF WE CAN'T AFFORD THE FUCKING MILITARY, LET'S GET RID OF IT! As of 2016, retired Presidents receive $450,000 a year for life, House and Senate members receive $174,000 a year for life, Speakers of the House receives $223,500 a year for the rest of their lives, Majority or Minority Leaders receive $194,400 per year for life, the average salary of a soldier deployed in Afghanistan is $38,000 a year, and, the average income for our Seniors on Social Security is $12,000 a year.

At the writing of this book, Republican Candidate Donald J. Trump claims that he will make America Great Again, and that he will cure our ills. In view of what is happening in American, he would be one of our busiest Presidents ever, should he become the President. In my opinion, since he is not a politician, he has a good shot at getting voters to buy into his rhetoric. We shall see. I do not think his promises will sit right with liberals, however.

Here is a true story of an abuse of RHIP, while managing the Officers Club as a civilian GS-11 at Williams Air Force Base, in Arizona, after the end of my military enlistment. Our Wing Commander was a full bird Colonel. His next promotion would be a one Star general if he passed the next Inspector General visit, which would move him to the Air Force Academy as the Commandant and as a one-star General. But here was a pure case of the abuse of <u>rank having its privileges</u>. He had the very best living quarters on the base; which I bear no heartburn. On a specific occasion, he had some visiting dignitaries and his officer friends, visiting the base. He told me to bring portable equipment into his quarters and provide a full course meal using some of my waitresses to serve and to have my chef cater the food. Could I say no to such a request? This is a blatant violation of protocol, <u>since no other dues-paying club member had any such privilege</u>. I'm not trying to be a rat in revealing this particular event, but the point needs to be made. <u>Where does this fine line of RHIP start and end?</u> The fact that he was the top officer of the base, nevertheless, did not give him such a privilege. By the way, he was assigned to The Air Force Academy later that year as a Brigadier General. If you don't break the rules, you are not going to get promoted! Well, that only applies to commissioned officers. Enlisted always pay the consequences for their rule breaking because <u>charges are always preferred by commissioned officers</u>. There I go again; sounding like I hate officers. Well, I hate the misfits I have eluded to, **but not the officers I respect and honor**. It took me 27 years to come across only a dozen or so good officers I was able to honor and respect. Any readers who might be an active duty or retired commissioned officer, and if you don't like the truth that I have exposed about the bad officers in the military, then get involved in a campaign to re-write the code as applies to officers to change all the bull shit to remove the king's crown a commissioned officer wears. As a career soldier, always ready to serve my country, I have a very bold statement to make, and that is; <u>RANK DOES NOT HAVE ITS PRIVILEGES, RATHER, IT HAS ITS RESPONSIBILITIES</u>! Get officers to buy into this, and we will have a strong officer corp.

By the way, it's refreshing when people say to me; when I wear my Vietnam baseball cap, "Thank you for your service". When I first returned from Vietnam, they said, "There goes another baby killer!" Little do Americans know what trials and tribulations the enlisted man must endure during his early years of service. They should pay attention to the suicides they are hearing about and ask questions to correct the reasons why they occur. Military Psychiatrists can't even figure it out. The reason why the Military Psychiatrists can't figure it out is because they need to go to these combat zones for a year, then come home for six months, then go back for a year! They will then learn the secret.

IF WE MUST MAINTAIN A MILITARY FORCE, THEN WE MUST THROW ALL THE TRADITIONAL HORSE SHIT OUT THE WINDOW AND DO SOMETHING TO BETTER COMPENSATE OUR FIGHTING MEN AND WOMEN. WHOSE GOING TO DO IT? THE PRESIDENT, CONGRESS, OUR ELECTED REPRESENTATIVES? I don't think so! If it's not your problem, then you don't care! If you don't care one way or another, then you are what perpetuates the average American's attitude of today. Patriotism is slowly dying; maybe I should say rapidly dying.

Back to Vietnam. On one of my trips delivering the Major just a few blocks outside the main gate of Tan Son Nhut Air Base, to the swank hotel where he resided, he asked me to come on up to the roof where we could have a drink together. There was a nice bar up there with tables and chairs. While fraternization was frowned upon stateside, it was totally ignored in Vietnam. Not only was it frowned upon but remains in the Manual for Courts Martial today under Article 134, as an offense! In essence, they made sure back in the day that an officer had a social status several rungs above an enlisted man, as an enlisted man was not worthy of sitting at the same table with an officer. Is this what the military should be all about? Military protocol mandates that familiarity breeds contempt. It is felt that a military man must fear and respect his officer counterparts in order for there to be discipline. That's funny, because in the civilian world, corporations thrive without all that bull shit because you know who your immediate supervisor is, and unless you are a natural born ASS KISSER, you are not required to kiss the ass of your supervisor, and you may sit at the same table with him or her. Sounds like I'm trying to change the military. I believe someone has to take that step. It will never happen within the military as changes to rid the service of RHIP would have to come from the civilian sector of our government. I call it, "The impossible dream".

After securing the Jeep in the hotel compound, the Major and I proceeded on into the hotel. At the front of the hotel door was two-armed military police and two Vietnamese police wearing white helmets whom we called, "WHITE MICE". We went to a table and a waitress built like a brick shit house came and took our order. I turned to the Major and said something like, "Are we still in a Combat Zone?" He laughed and said,

"Sarge, this is how I forget the war every night!" He had the hots for this waitress and after work, she lived with him in his room. So here, Uncle Sam was providing a whore house for a commissioned officer, but none for an enlisted man. Hell, we liked pussy too! As we were having our second drink, I noticed three young army PFC's at a table. I asked the Major if anybody could come into the hotel to the bar on the roof to which he replied,

"No, they always come in with their Captain, but I guess he went down to his room. The next thing I heard was this young punk Army private, who was obviously drunk on his ass, and standing on top of the table where he and two others were seated, yelling,

"I'm 173rd Army Airborne, and I want to kill gooks and Air Force faggots." He was smiling when looking over at the only two Air Force guys in the place; me and the Major, then raised his pistol and shot a few rounds into the air. My Major got up and said, "Let's go down to my room before this idiot shoots somebody!" I then said, "Fuck no, I'm not going to let this punk intimidate me or you; that's what's wrong with the discipline in Vietnam!" With this, I got up and walked slowly towards the kid standing on the table. The Major said, "What are you trying to do, get another Bronze Star, or go home in a box?" Walking closer to the kid, I said, "Hey 173rd Airborne, we like what you guys do in the field, and we are all proud of you!" As I saw his raised gun come down slowly, thinking the son of a bitch was going to shoot me, he held it down to his side and said, "Hey Air Force, sit down with us and let us buy you a drink." I then said, "Do me a favor. Let me have your weapon, and I'll let them hold it behind the bar. My Major is not well and might be going home soon. He has become very upset over your shooting." He looked over at the Major sitting three tables away, and looked at me handing me his pistol, which I brought to the bartender. I sat down and had to have at least three more drinks with the Army dudes. I was getting a little drunk at this point. I told them I was going back to the table where the Major was sitting. We shook hands and that ended that saga. When I got to the Major, he looked at me, starred for a good minute, and said, "Sarge; you are a crazy bastard! He might have blown your head off for Christ sake!" I replied, "Yeah, but he didn't. So maybe you could get me another Bronze Star?" He said, "Bronze Star hell, I'm going to put you in for the Psycho Award!"

The ten o'clock curfew was almost upon us, so it was time for me to scurry back to the base. The Major asked me to pick him up at nine in the morning. I was at work at seven but picked him up at nine. It took me a couple of days to relive that situation on the roof of the hotel, before I was able to calm down and get it off my brain. This is one of those events I eluded to where, the longer you are in Vietnam, the more you did stupid things.

That night, there was a movie in that open compound I eluded too earlier. While watching the movie, the damn siren went off. Everyone was running like hell to their favorite death traps. I just slowly walked toward the NCO Club. The next thing I recall; I was being picked up by two Army African American privates. While everyone was scurrying all over the place to safety, these guys nevertheless stuck with me. When they stood me up, the whole world was going upside down and I fell to the ground. They were talking to me, but I could not hear them. The only thing I could hear was a loud ringing in my ears. After a few minutes, as the ringing subsided, my hearing was coming back.

My vertigo was still with me. I asked them what happened to which they informed me, that a nearby rocket explosion knocked me at least 30 yards away. I told them that I never heard an explosion or anything. They got me to the dispensary a block away where I was examined and released. For several days after, my vertigo was coming and going and I could not control it. My back was killing me. My hearing was impaired to the point that, if I wasn't looking straight at you, I could not make out your words. There was nothing wrong with the volume I was hearing, but what I was hearing had a base sound and was muffled to me. I wanted to get the problem solved, but the doctor at the base dispensary said they would have to send me to Hawaii for tests, and back stateside after that. I requested we wait a bit to see if it would subside. When my boss heard what I wanted to do he said,

"Hell, you will probably get the purple heart for this, and you can get the hell out of here." I replied,

"Major, this is my first assignment as NCOIC. It's a necessary foundation to the steps of being a qualified Legal Specialist. Besides, the guys at the office are depending on me, and I don't want to let them down.".

When you were in Vietnam at the six-month point, you could either go to Hawaii or Australia for a week and the military would get you to either place. I chose Hawaii and had my wife and two-year-old daughter join me for my R&R (Rest and Recooperation). When I was at the Honolulu Airport trying to find my wife and daughter, something began tugging on my pants leg saying, "Daddy, Daddy". I looked down and saw that my daughter did not forget me, bringing tears to my eyes. The next thing a hand was on my shoulder; it was my wife. After about thirty minutes with them, I said to my wife,

"Thank God, her stuttering has stopped." My wife shocked me by saying,

"On the plane, when I told her we were going to see Daddy, she started talking without stuttering."

I was shocked again. The hardest thing of my life was leaving them in Hawaii, and then going back to HELL for another six months, but I did it. What we all said while in Vietnam was, for example, if you were going home in 86 days, we would say, "I have 85 days and a wake-up!" Then some wisecracker would say, "What if you don't wake up?"

I did my best to keep up my morale for the remainder of my tour in Nam. I never told my wife about my rocket experience causing vertigo and hearing impairment. I never went back to the dispensary (hospital) for my condition and took the secret all the way to my discharge ten years later. Even today, most of the time, when my wife says something, I follow up with "WHAT".

I had about 5 days and a wake-up to go. While walking toward my buddy to get him to go to chow with me, I heard a funny noise like somebody broke a piece of wood. He was on a top bunk. I went over to my buddy's upper bunk where he was reading a letter from his wife and yelled at him,

"Hey butt head, get your ass out of bed, and let's go to chow." He didn't move, nor did he respond. I walked up to the side of the bed and saw that a letter was lying on his face with blood on it. I removed the letter and saw that his eyes were wide open and he had a bullet hole in his forehead. The bullet had rica-shade off the square wooden post by his bed and went into his head. He never knew what hit him. <u>Man, my horse shit Vietnam events were piling up as memories that would haunt me for a long time via dreams and nightmares</u>. If you think that the combat military who have been deemed to have PTSD are full of shit, then you live on Mars. I finally had to move into another bedroom from my wife when I returned home, because I usually swung my arms around during bad dreams and thought I might accidentally hit her. I've been sleeping there ever since!

Many crazy things transpired while in the Nam for a year. One day, this two-striper airman came into our office for legal assistance. As he was leaving, he noticed that behind me, there was a framed large picture of a C-130 Hercules airplane. He looked at it and said, "Sarge, I work on the C-130s and I'd like to have that picture; what will you take for it?" I asked him what he had to trade. He said, "I have an oscillating fan attached to the post by my bed I'll trade you for it." I said, "Just what I'm looking for; bring it to me, and you can have the picture." In the NAM we traded each other for the craziest things we did or didn't need. I bought a bike from a guy who was going back to the states for $5 bucks. I sold it a week later for $20 bucks.

CHAPTER 6

The next event I am about to reveal was the top trade of all trades while I was in the Nam. My Major, used the Jeep one day, and went down to Saigon to shop at the commissary. He couldn't find me, so he elected to go alone. When he came out of the commissary, the Jeep was gone. The Base Commander had announced the week before that too many vehicles were being stolen due to negligence, and that the next vehicle that was stolen would result in the Court Martial of the idiot who lost it, including paying for the vehicle. My boss, took a cab back to the base. Would you believe a cab in a combat zone? He came into the office looking for me, but I was at my hooch. He came to the hooch and was as white as a sheet when telling me what had happened. I told him not to report it to the commander and give me 24 hours to try something. We walked back to the office, just one block away, and we got the envelope from the Major's desk that was like a registration with the Jeep numbers and showing it was assigned to the Legal Office.

"You aren't going to do anything illegal are you?" I answered, "Nothing as illegal as you did when you failed to secure the Jeep which caused it to be stolen." He looked at me and smiled.

I got on the phone and called my buddy at the Base Mess Hall. I told him that I needed a case of T-Bone Steaks telling him that I would need it for an important horse trade, reminding him that he owed me a big favor. He assured me that he would put a hold on a case in their freezer.

Next, I called my buddy who was the NCOIC of the Motor Pool. After explaining about the stolen Jeep, he asked me if I had the numbers from the hood of the Jeep so that he could stencil our original numbers on the hood of a new Jeep in the motor pool compound. He asked what I would give him in return to which I told him that he could have a case of T-Bone Steaks. Now a case was about 60 pounds of steaks. He jumped at it because his outfit was planning a hot dog and hamburger cook out. The Steaks really appealed to him and would make him a hero. The next morning, I went to the hotel to pick up the Major. He was about to call a cab. I reiterate, can you believe calling a cab in a Combat Zone? When he came outside and saw the new Jeep, he looked at me and said, "Is this our Jeep?" I replied, "No sir, it's <u>my Jeep</u> because you don't know how to secure a Jeep off base." He laughed at this and said, "Sarge, where do you get these ideas to pull something off like this?" I replied, "Sir, what I do is always by pure survival instincts; nothing else! I grew up in a tough town, called Hoboken, in New Jersey. Plus, I was a race driver before entering the service and learned to react without thought." Something that you had to be very careful of with a Jeep was; the gas cap of the Jeep was large enough to stick your fist into the tank. If you were in an area off the base, the VC would send a little kid with a grenade that the pin had been pulled, but the trigger was being held by strong wide rubber bands. The way this trick worked, when the gas in the tank finally deteriorated the rubber bands, the Jeep would explode.

Sometimes people would be in it, and sometimes not. These bastards could create more havoc with a <u>dimes worth of material</u> than anybody in the world. I had a heavy steel ring welded to the gas cap, and ran a chain through the ring, pulling it tight and chaining it to a ring welded to the floor using a large Pad Lock on the chain. My good buddy at the motor pool did this for me. Now it was virtually impossible to loosen the gas cap because you could barely turn the cap at all. This pleased the Major.

Like an idiot, with 3 days and a wake up left on my Vietnam vacation, yes, like an idiot, I had an Army friend, who was one of the guys who picked me up from the rocket explosion, and who was on perimeter patrol; you know, perimeter, the chain link around the base that protects us; <u>not?</u> He stopped by my hootch and asked me to walk around the perimeter with him as he was on duty to do the walk. Since it might be the last time we would see each other, I accompanied him. He said if anything popped up in front of us, shoot and ask questions later. Now I'm wondering, I need to be doing this 3 days before I am going home? Within ten minutes or so, shots were fired into our direction. The Army dude, being smarter than I, hit the deck, and with my M-16 on automatic, I sprayed the person in front of us. It was a VC young kid about 16 years old, who worked his way on to the base. Yes, I killed him. The first person in my entire life whom I had ever killed. It didn't matter that he was the enemy VC, what mattered was that he was a human being, and a kid about the age of my sons. At the writing of this book, which I keep repeating, is now 2016, the fact that I am revealing it, is still upsetting to me. Maybe this is part of my PTSD. I guess it really is one of the problems that haunts me. Another thing that haunts me is the fact that our office was right next to the Base Morgue. Daily, when I would get my buddy who worked there to go to chow, I made a walkthrough. I'll never forget that the dead were on a wooden platform that was leaning against the wall on an angle. I saw no old dead people, they were all kids, for Christ sake. There were many times that the morgue people would put white sheets on the ground outside and open body bags. They would take pieces of bodies and try putting them together like a jig saw puzzle. When they found a jawbone that fit most of the pieces, they now had a person's identification. I have to tell you that the stench at all times next to our office was that of dead bodies, and the strong odor of formaldehyde. This was a nice odor to take to the mess hall with you. I remember seeing young kids who didn't have a mark on them, but who died from a strong explosive concussion. I was informed by my morgue buddy that a majority of these deaths were from concussive explosions without making a mark on their bodies. During one of my idiotic evaluations at the VA, I related this event to the evaluator. A month later, I got a copy of his report. <u>Here is what he wrote:</u>

"This veteran relates that he had Morgue duties while in Vietnam and that he had to put pieces of bodies together for identification purposes." Certainly, I had to contest this to have it corrected. <u>God, these people were all brain dead at the VA!</u>

A night that shall always stand out in my mind is when the hut two doors from my hut got a direct hit from a rocket. Since the siren was blowing, everybody was scurrying like a herd of wild animals. Me and my morgue buddy went to the hut that was hit. It became obvious that perhaps half of the men were dead. It was horrible as the screaming of injured was as loud as the siren that was still going off. My buddy and I saw life in several of the men, and, using the fireman's carry, we carried about six of them down to the hospital a block away. Some of those survived, while some did not. Did I have nightmares for a long time? I still have them occasionally. Here again, upon revealing this incident to an evaluator at the VA, **here is what he wrote:**

"The veteran states that he had to go into burning buildings often to rescue people from a rocket blast."

Yes, I had that thrown out, like everything else. I guess they were bad note takers, but hell, **they were recording it!**

Although there were numerous incidents that I would like to forget, one of the happiest things I recall was; **leaving Vietnam**! There could not, at that moment, be anything in the world that would be better. In coming home, we flew into the Philippines first, then to Hawaii, then to San Francisco. My buddies did their best to get me shit faced drunk for my farewell party just before boarding the plane. I got so damn drunk that they had to hold me up on both sides and put me in my seat. I then awakened when I heard this loud scream the minute the planes wheels left the ground of Vietnam. The lifting of the wheels meant that you were not killed in the NAM, and it was something to cheer about. After that, I slept the 910 miles and woke up in Manila. I found out about a month after leaving that one of the guys who helped pour me on the airplane was killed by a rocket explosion in one of those **SELF-MADE DEATH TRAP BUNKERS**! Damn, how unnecessary, because Uncle Sam didn't see fit to provide adequate, or any for that matter, bunkers for our troops. Here is where the officers had it made. The enemy rocketed the base, not the Swanky Hotels and Villas downtown where the officers lived.

After Vietnam, my assignment was to Colorado Springs, Colorado, at the Base Legal Office where I stayed for almost three years. My boss said that the Base Commander wanted to see me. I now had three years of college under by belt because of burning the midnight oil in classes at night and weekends. When I got to his office, he had a set of stripes in his hand telling me that I had been promoted to Senior Master Sergeant. He then said,

"Sarge, I have an opportunity you might be interested in. The Morale, Welfare, and Recreation field have a need for high-ranking NCOs; specifically, in the military club field. Would you have any interest in changing career fields? Would you like the challenge at this stage of your career?" I answered,

"Sir, my studies in college have been hospitality orientated, which covers finance, club, and hotel management. I would welcome the challenge."

The rest was history. I was sent three weeks later to Lowry Air Force Base, Colorado, just 70 miles north to Denver at the Military Club Management School. The school was a snap and I graduated at the very top of the class. My college hospitality studies certainly made that possible. The Air Force sent me to advanced studies such as Michigan State for a summer semester on culinary techniques, and Cornell University for studies on Financial Management. They certainly prepared me for my new career field, and I loved it.

My first job after graduation was at the NCO Club at Fairchild Air Force Base, in Spokane, Washington. The club was in a losing mode for several months prior to my arrival. During my first year as manager of the club, we went into the black. Because of my rank and my immediate success with my first club, I was selected for an assignment at HQ PACAF, in Hawaii. In this job, working directly under a Major and a Colonel, I was overseer of 42 officer and enlisted night clubs throughout the Pacific Theatre. When I make reference to Military Clubs; a club is, in essence, a night club with a Bar, a Restaurant, and weekend entertainment. We had clubs in bases in Japan, South Korea, Thailand, Taiwan, Guam, Kwajalein Atoll, and clubs right there in Hawaii. It was my job to monitor all of their financial statements every month to evaluate problems. The problems at the time were that 18 of the 42 clubs in the Pacific were operating in the red. This was a bad spot for my Colonel to be in, since he was the head of all PACAF clubs in the Pacific. By the way, he was one of the good officers I eluded too earlier. The taxpayers were not willing to pay for the military to have a night club any longer, so if you are going to have one, it must pay its own way by being in the black financially. The PACAF Commander; a one-star General, didn't want these glitches because, damn; he only had one star and certainly wanted another one, but he was absolutely very mission oriented. Everything in the military is based upon performance. My Colonel, called me into his office and asked me if I had been reviewing the financial statements, and asked what I thought about the 18 clubs in the red. I answered,

"Sir, I have thoroughly studied them, and I have definitely come to some conclusions as to what is going on." He asked what my conclusions were. I told him,

"Knowing the temptations that are available to Club Managers and their assistants, they are robbing the clubs blind in more ways than one." This certainly got his interest. He then buzzed the Major, who was my immediate supervisor, and asked him to come into his office. He then said, "Major, have you been reviewing the financials of the clubs in the field?" The major answered in the affirmative. The Colonel then said, "Do you have any remedies for the clubs in the red?" The major answered, "Sir, traditionally, there have always been twelve to twenty of the forty-two clubs teetering in the red. Nobody has been able to solve that problem for the past three years." To my amazement the Colonel then said, "I want you to get orders for Sergeant Berry to visit the clubs at all the bases we have for evaluation purposes, and to find a way to get these clubs out of the red." The Major then said in an annoying tone, "Sir, Sergeant Berry has only been in the Club Field for a year. I don't see what magic he might be able to come up with for a solution to a problem that has gone on for over three years during my tour here." The Colonel then said, "Maybe when he returns you can find out something you hadn't learned over the past three years. Sarge, I'll send Lt. Colonel Williams with you. He is a good Morale, Welfare man, but not a club man. He will be glad to work with you."

For three days before leaving for the Far East, the Major did not speak one word to me. I could tell he disliked my cocky confidence. I do have to admit that I was a very cocky guy proud of my experiences and my accomplishments and felt that no challenge could be too demanding for me. Maybe I thought too much of myself. But I used my cockiness to my advantage to get the mission accomplished. Finally, the day after my return from the Pacific Clubs, about 30 days later, the Major came to me and said,

"Sarge, come into my office for a minute. I want to speak to you <u>off the record</u>." He then said rather sarcastically, "I don't like your report on your visit to the bases in the Far East, and further, I want you to re-write it, and I'll dictate to you how I want it to read. There is too much information that the General would not be happy about reading, especially since he had never heard about the things you have revealed. It kind of makes me look like an idiot." I then said, "Major, why the hell did they send me out there to bases in the Pacific if the General didn't want the truth about what was going on?" He replied, "You don't like officers, do you?" I answered, "What the hell does that have to do with this? But in answer to your question; No, I have no respect for officers when they are like you Major!" He then added, "Are you trying your hand at insubordination now?" I said, "What the hell happened to "OFF THE RECORD", are you afraid of where this is going?" He came back with, "OK, we're off the record. What specifically is it you dislike about me?" I answered, "All you care about Major, is making Lt. Colonel, and there is nothing wrong with that except that you don't mind doing it at the risk of whomever might be in your way! You want the General to have the mistaken belief that everything is working out fine in the field, and that 18 our 42 clubs in the red is a normal occurrence, and you would like me to assist you in that lie. Well, forget it; you can't order me to tell a lie, and if you change my report, I will go directly to the General to tell him what a fucking phony you are! Do you still want to stay off the record; SIR?" With this, the Major slapped his hand down on the desk and ended our session, realizing that he lost the battle. I think he must have learned never to go "off the record" with a ranking NCO.

It was time for my yearly fitness report. When it was completed by the Major who was my first-line supervisor, the report, which I am obliged to acknowledge by signing it below his signature, was the biggest bunch of bull shit I had ever witnessed. It solidified my feeling about him as being the poorest Officer I had ever served under. Absolutely the poorest! I got up and walked right into the Colonel's office. I placed the report on his desk and said, "Colonel, your Major thinks I am the most uncooperative NCO he has ever witnessed. He further feels that I do not conform to the standards of the missions I go out on. He also wants to blow smoke up the General's ass, and he wants to re-write my report. What do you think sir?" He buzzed the Major without saying a word to me, and to my great surprise he said to the Major, "What the hell is this piece of shit? This man is the best damn NCO I have ever been associated with. Your rating of him will be tossed, and I will rate him personally and have our one-star General endorse it. I believe the General does not share your opinion either. From this point on Sergeant Berry comes directly under myself and the General; you're out of the loop!"

I was quite aware of numerous enlisted men whose career progress was stopped because of assholes like the Major, and I was not going to let him do it to me. I worked hard and dedicated myself to every mission. Lt. Colonel Williams who accompanied me on our mission in the Pacific said with a smile,

"Good for you Bob."

This meant a lot to me because I had great respect for him as a man and an Officer of the United States Air Force. The next morning, I had to review my trip report with the Colonel as the next step was for us to brief the General. He stated, "Sarge, your report was very candid, unlike the whitewashed ones I have been accustomed to seeing. Lt. Colonel Williams said you stayed on the job relentlessly and had great respect from the club managers at the various clubs. It is quite evident that you discovered that the clubs in the red are those that are being neglected by the managers. Your indication that they are not only stealing from the tills but that when they hire entertainment, the check is written out as a cost of $500. For the band, while the band hands the club manager $100. Cash for his pocket. You also state that they sleep around with the oriental waitresses. With charges like this, perhaps we need to get OSI (Office of Special Investigations) involved for investigations with a view toward prosecution. What do you think?" I said, "Yes sir, we could do that, but this would not get the clubs out of the red during the remainder of your tour in Hawaii, and I believe that I can get them all out of the red before that if you let me present a proposition to the General. By the time OSI investigations are completed, the guys would be back in the states at another club, so getting OSI involved would be counterproductive. If I could do it my way and have total control, I could get the bad guys out of the club field after their return to the states, while sending them to the base of their choice upon their return." The Colonel then said, how the heck are you going to accomplish this?" I said,

"Sir, let's you and I go to the General where I will lay it all out, then I won't have to explain it twice. He will either throw us out of his office or kiss us and give us candy. He's a damn good officer and a guy who uses logic to make his decisions. What do we have to lose?"

At the General's office, here is what I proposed,

"General, if you get me total authority from Randolph Air Force Base, Texas, to transfer their authority to me for assignments of club managers in and out of the Pacific Theatre, and let me bring all of our PACAF Club Managers to Hawaii for a conference, I will work some magic. My plan is to tell them that if they get their clubs out of the red and maintain progress by staying in the black from the time that they leave Hawaii to go back to their bases, all the way to the time that they leave for their stateside assignment, I will let them chose the base they wish to return to, but not unless this provision is completely met. There is no better dangling bate sir in the whole world than giving a man his choice of a base upon return to the mainland." The General chuckled, then said, "That's a big order, Sarge. I don't believe Randolph has ever relinquished their assignment authority, nor do I know if they can. Sounds like you might just have something there; let me get on it. I am a personal friend of the Randolph Base Personnel Officer. I'll get on it today and let you know how we make out. How long do you want to have this authority? I replied, "Just from now until I return to the states at my next assignment."

Two days later, the General called me and the Colonel to his office. He said, "Sarge, you got the power! We are going to set up a CTR computer at your desk so that you can coordinate and bring men in from the states to replace the men whose tours of duty are up here in the Pacific Theatre. You will have a direct line to Randolph Assignments. You can send the PACAF Club managers to whatever bases you desire. I have also approved bringing the managers to a conference here for five days. What else do you need?" I asked, "Sir, do I have the power to have them removed from the club field upon their arrival at their stateside duty station without prejudice so that they can go on to a job that might be useful to the Air Force?" The General said jokingly, "Sarge, why ask; you now have more power than I have!"

For months, the Major, watching me work the system, always looked at me like he would like to shoot me. I can't say I blamed him. I looked back at him with daggers also and never spoke a word to him. He also saw the clubs emerge from the red into the black one by one. He should have been happy for our mission being on the right track, but he didn't really give a damn. He was certainly jealous. Usually, people on the Morale, Welfare and Recreation side of the house were envious of club people and although we were under the one umbrella, we were miles apart.

To make a long story short, when my tour of duty ended in Hawaii, all 42 clubs were in the black. This was good for the Colonel, and the General. For this, I was given a special award. The Major disliked me because he had not been able to accomplish this in his three-year tour of duty. The real reason for that was that he was not a man of Club background as he was just a Morale, Welfare, Recreation man. I met up with the Major about four years later, and noticed that he was a full bird colonel. So, how he got two promotions to that level in four years will always be a joke to me. He was a rather clever guy though. As a matter of fact, he was a very clever guy.

CHAPTER 7

It was now the end of my Hawaii tour and I would be leaving for a stateside assignment in a few weeks. I received a phone call from Randolph Air Force Base, in Texas. It was the NCO, a Chief Master Sergeant, who was formally in charge of the club manager's assignments. He said that, he now had control again of the club people's assignments and congratulated me for what I had pulled off in Hawaii in getting the clubs back in the black. He then went on to say, "By the way, you have been promoted to the highest rank in the Air Force; Chief Master Sergeant and I congratulate you for that also. But I have some news for you. I was informed that you are from Florida, and would like to be assigned there; is that true?" I replied that I would like nothing better. He then said, "Since you are a master at getting clubs out of the red, how would you like to go to Patrick Air Force Base, in Cocoa Beach, Florida. The NCO Club happens to be <u>the worse club</u> <u>in the entire Air Force</u>. They are $40,000 in the red with six months to go to the end of the year. The club manager was fired by the Base Commander. When he made inquiries to our big MWR boss in Texas for special help in getting a hot shot to his base, your name came up as the man for the job. I told Randolph that I hated to stick you with the worse club in the Air force after the great job you did at PACAF, but figured you would be up for the challenge. I replied,

"Chief; I would love the challenge." Needless to say, my wife was very pleased that we would be going to Florida for perhaps the final job before my retirement.

Upon arriving at the Patrick Air Force Base, Cocoa Beach, Florida, NCO Club, I took an immediate liking to all of the civilian staff working there. They were all expertise in their jobs and were waiting for some kind of guidance. Two lower ranking enlisted men were also assigned to the club but had no club training. All they were good at was taking end of month inventory of food and daily inventory of liquor. I had everyone come in an hour before opening time the following day for my introductory talk with them. I had breakfast catered in by a civilian firm which shocked everyone. My talk with them went something like this:

"Folks; as your new manager, while I know you are accustomed to a new manager coming in to make changes and attempt to overhaul the operation, this will not be my mission. From my observation, I am confident with the entire operation. It appears that there is much to do as we are $40,000 in the red. It is my mission however to find out why we are losing money, and how I can increase our membership. My door is open, and I am always open for ideas. Keep up the good work."

Amazingly, of the 12 employees that were assigned to the club, all 12 came into my office one at a time giving me tremendous insight and good ideas to increase membership. Basically, I was told that, the club being right on the Atlantic Ocean, was surrounded with all kinds of night clubs and eating places, and that the previous manager increased the prices to offset the losses, and minimized the menu items, but nothing worked. I then sent the two young airmen ten miles north and 10 miles south along the A1A ocean highway to go to places and give me total details on what these places do, what they serve, and told them to steal menus. The older airman of the two said,

"Chief, I'm not sure what you will expect to accomplish by us doing this. It should take us at least a week to do what you ask." I replied with,

"The best thing you guys can do is have total faith in me. We will accomplish much if you do exactly as I ask and do it in the most professional way that you are capable of doing. The first thing to do is remove all your negativity and be ready for things that you have not seen in this club during your assignment here."

With the input from these two guys, which was greater than I expected, I was able to revise our menu and make our prices lower than the competition. I gave free Steak Night to members in good standing every Tuesday night, and free Spaghetti night every Friday. In addition, I created a Sunday buffet which I knew our people were capable of carrying out. I lowered monthly dues from $14.00 a month to $8.00 a month. Within the first month, membership increased an amazing 30%. Even though the dues were lowered, the increase in membership actually created greater dues income and greater revenue. My goal was to use members' dues to pay for the free food nights and to increase entertainment. I inserted a piano bar during the week, and a band on Friday and Saturday. The club was always packed from here on out. At the end of the fiscal year, we eliminated the $40,000 deficit and finished the year $22,000 in the black; representing a $62,000 turnaround.

I was informed that a Colonel from Morale, Welfare, and Recreation, was coming from headquarters in San Antonio, Texas, to present me with an award for my accomplishment. To my surprise, it was the famous Major from Hawaii, who was now a full bird Colonel. For him to have to come to Florida to present me with an award they called, "The Air Force Excellence Award," had to be downright degrading to him. Surprisingly, we greeted each other cordially, shook hands, and he surprised me further by saying,

"I must admit that by turning the Air Force's worst club in the Air Force, to the most profitable club in the Air Force, is a most astounding achievement. I congratulate you on a most outstanding accomplishment, and I shall now read your award. He read,

"In a field where successful operation depends on the initiative of the manager, the NCO Club at Patrick Air Force Base is recognized as the best club in Air Force Systems Command. For your high degree of professionalism in club management, this award is hereby presented to Chief Master Sergeant Robert Berry." With this, he shook my hand, and I rendered him a salute.

During a military career, one has to become hardened to the many ups and downs, together with the many hardships along the way. Having survived it all, I am thankful for having had the opportunity to find out if I had something to contribute. I shall never forget the career and the many experiences that challenged me.

The military has done more for me than I did for it. I was able to attain my hospitality college degree and was afforded the best training possible by the Air Force.

Upon my discharge from the Air Force, my resume was good enough to land me a job as General Manager of the Sheraton Regency Resort Hotel, right on the ocean at Vero Beach, Florida. This was another one of those losing scenarios. The Hotel lost $175,000 the previous year and was looking for a miracle man to turn things around. When I interviewed for the job, the franchise owner, asked me what kind of a salary I was looking to receive. He then asked me if I thought I could turn things around. I told him, I didn't think I could turn it around, but knew I could turn it around on one condition. He asked me what that condition was, and I told him,

"Mr. Cocolin, I have been informed by the employees of this hotel that you are an interfering son of a bitch, when it comes to a manager trying to do his job. You need to let go completely and give me a free hand. I don't want to hear about employees complaining about me to you. I want you to tell them that <u>I AM IN TOTAL CONTROL</u>. Go back to Pennsylvania and watch over your interests there. If I don't have total control without interference, then I don't want the job." He then said,

"OK, I'll give you what you ask. Now let's talk about salary." I said,

"I want 10% of the bottom-line improvement, and a base salary of $60,000 a year."

I really didn't want the job because Vero Beach Florida was about 40 miles from my home in Indian Harbor Beach. Surprisingly he said,

"OK, at the end of the first six months, we'll see if you made your 10% of the bottom-line improvement. I'm leaving in the morning. Are you ready to take over?" I indicated that I was ready.

At the end of the first six months, I was handed a $10,000 check for my bottom-line improvement which meant, in essence, that we were looking at a $100,000 profit halfway through the year. I won't get into all the ways that I was able to accomplish this except to say that my disappointment came when I found out that he was selling the hotel to an Iranian family, thanks to my bottom-line convincer. I completed my one-year contract and declined to work for the Iranians when they took over at the beginning of the year, because I would have had to supervise, Mom, Pop, Daughters, Sons, Uncles, Aunts, and Grandparents. I am now totally retired at 84 years old and enjoying life with my wife of over 51 years.

CHAPTER 8

Years after my discharge from the Air Force in 1979, I received a letter from the Veteran's Administration in Phoenix, Arizona, telling me that they were screening Vietnam veterans for a variety of reasons. I reported and was shocked over the session I had with an evaluator who was a Psychiatrist. He was older than dirt and should have been in a rest home or somewhere he could be happy. I angrily remember how bad our interview had gone. The evaluator said,

"Mr. Berry, do you know why you are here for this evaluation?" I said sarcastically,

"You tell me; I was told to report and discuss some of the problems I was having since my discharge. He then said,

"I see here where you claim to be having bad dreams that you suffer from occasional vertigo, that you have some numbness in the upper part of your legs. It also says here that you are a type two diabetic, and that you have had your cancerous prostate removed. It also seems to me that you are having trouble due to your PTSD." I answered,

"I never heard of PTSD. What is it?" He replied,

"It stands for post-traumatic stress disorder. It is usually the final result of one's experiences with terrifying events that can cause on-going mental anguish. However, in your case, I am puzzled as to why you would be experiencing any of the usual symptoms, since your service in Vietnam in 1968 and 1969 was many years ago. Certainly, you would not be going through mental anguish after all this time. Can you explain your PTSD to me?" I then said,

"Doctor, I never said I had PTSD. I have a lot of questions for you though!" He said,

"No, it is I who will be asking the questions." I then blurted back,

"Like hell you will! You're going to listen to my questions, or you will be explaining to someone higher up why you are unable to conduct a one-on-one session rather than the one-sided session you prefer! When I finish, then you can ask your damn questions. He then turned his chair toward the window. Seeing this, then I said,

"What the hell kind of an interrogator are you? How about giving me the God Damn courtesy of looking at me while I talk to you, like I was looking at you straight in the eye when you were speaking to me?" He just shrugged his shoulders. What an ass hole! So, I proceeded on with my questions to him saying,

"You don't have to answer any of my questions, but just listen and absorb them for posterity. Question one is, "Did you ever shoot and kill a person"? NO? I did!" Question two, "How many rocket attacks did you ever experience wondering if one had your fucking name on it?" Question three, "WHEN THE HELL ARE YOUR EVALUATORS GOING TO BELIEVE THAT VETERANS ARE NOT FAKING TO RECEIVE DISABILITY COMPENSATION?" The doctor then said,

"Sir, it sounds to me like you are a strong candidate for a PTSD evaluation, and I shall recommend it. Thank you for your patience and thank you for your service." Boy, what an ass hole I was with this old gentleman. I later felt bad about my conduct at that session. About a month later, I was to report for a PTSD evaluation at the Phoenix VA. This time, it was a different evaluator. He didn't greet me, or say I am Doctor so and so, but merely said, "Have a seat." I then said,

"Well, you know who I am, how about telling me who you are?" He obliged me and we got started immediately on the wrong foot as he said, "I see that you believe you have PTSD." I then said,

"No, one of your screwball doctors said that he believed that! I then said, "I see that we are going to have a problem with this evaluation!" He then said,

"No, we are not going to have any problems. Just calmly answer my questions to aid me in my evaluation." I said that I would, and we proceeded to the first stupid question when he said, "I see that you received a medal called the Bronze Star while in Vietnam. Is it a combat medal?" I then said angrily, "Jesus Christ, are you trying to piss me off to see how I will react? If you don't know that a Bronze Star is a medal awarded for above and beyond the call of duty while engaging hostile enemy forces, you shouldn't be here doing these evaluations on veterans!" He then said,

"Well, I'm sorry, it's not listed here on my information sheet. OK, ok, so you have a combat medal! So, let's talk about your diabetes and prostate cancer. Do you contend that you should receive compensation for these conditions which are conditions that numerous people have who have never been in the service?" I then said,

"Man are you behind the fucking eight ball! Why is it that you are not aware that the government has conceded that anyone who was in Vietnam during their large-scale defoliation, which was the result of spraying a chemical known as Agent Orange, has been deemed to be the direct cause of both Diabetes and Prostate Cancer, to name a few?" He answered,

"Sorry, I've only been here a week, and haven't had time to catch up with all the required information; I never heard of Agent Orange!"

So, I had an evaluator who did not know that a Bronze Star was a combat medal, and who never heard of Agent Orange and its deadly ramifications. Oh, oh, here I go again;

"THANK YOU UNCLE SAM FOR THESE INTELLIGENT EVALUATORS!" The evaluator then asked me, "Are you currently receiving any disability compensation for these problems?" I said, "I received my first disability check two months ago in the amount of $642." He muttered,

"Oh, that's good." I then said,

"No, that's not good! After receipt of that, my retirement check was reduced by $642 dollars. I found out, in essence, that I was paying for my own God Damn disability! I notified the Armed Services Committee in Washington and found out that they were not aware of such a procedure. Good old Representative Sanford D. Bishop Jr. got on his horse and was able to get his house bill 333 passed that revoked this practice. Another example of how uninformed our representatives remain until something jolts them!" The evaluator then said,

"Are you still suffering from occasional vertigo and numbness in your legs?" My answer was,

"Yes, I am. Sometimes I can't stand for over five minutes without my thighs becoming very numb. My vertigo comes and goes whenever it wants to. While it is not severe, it has caused me to fall several times and I tore my rotator cuff in the process. He then said,

"What makes you feel that these problems are service connected?" I replied,

"Doctor, let me put it this way. Since the government has conceded that Agent Orange causes Diabetes and Prostate Cancer, I shouldn't have to tell you that neuropathy of the lower extremities is a direct result of diabetes. The vertigo is another story." He then said,

"Your records reflect that you were the victim of a close by rocket explosion which caused ringing in your ears, and occasional vertigo. Are you saying that after all these years, you are still experiencing these symptoms?" I said,

"It has been determined by my civilian primary care doctor that I have <u>irreparable ear damage</u>. I sent that report to the VA and it should be in your file. I have waited long enough for the VA to assign the proper disability award for these problems. As it stands, they will owe me retroactive pay from the time I first submitted my claim to now!" He then said,

"Ok. I'm going to have to set you up for a vertigo and hearing test, and for tests on your legs. It should be within the next 30 days."

At the test for vertigo and hearing, it became obvious that I could not keep my eyes closed while standing for any length of time without losing my balance. The hearing test proved that I could hear sounds but voices sounded muffled. I was diagnosed as having both presbyopia, an aging type of hearing loss, and <u>Noise-Induced hearing loss</u> which was the result of my exposure to the noise and impact of the nearby rocket explosion. They determined that this type of hearing loss could not be medically or surgically corrected. Their attempt to fit me with hearing aids did not cure the muffled sounds I was hearing. If I look at one's lips as they speak, everything is fine between what I see, and what I hear.

The next test at the VA was for the purpose of checking my thigh numbness. I was warned by a friend that they used electric shock testing. The doctor was oriental; perhaps Chinese. He had a very heavy accent and appeared to be out of his fucking head while he giggled. He greeted me and asked me to lie on the table on my stomach. He then hooked up an electrical shock device but was having difficulty getting it to work. He called in a corpsman who assisted him in getting it ready for the test. The next thing that happened was the feeling that I was being electrocuted, as he moved the device over the back of my legs. I had to ask,

"Doctor, what the hell are you doing at the back of my legs?" He said, "I check my leg for being numb. No worry, I no hurt you." I then said, "The fucking numbness is in front on my thighs, not the back of my legs!" He then said, "I check your leg in front now." Using his magic wand, he shocked the living hell out of me and then said, "Don't look like numb on front legs to me!"

Knowing this was going to happen, I had a large safety pin in my pocket. I pinched the skin up on my thigh between my thumb and index finger about an inch and stuck the pin through the raised skin and closed the safety pin. I then looked over at him with a smile to see his wide-eyed reaction. He then said, "Oh, oh, look like you do have some numb leg." Oh, oh; "THANK YOU UNCLE SAM FOR HAVING ANOTHER IDIOT EXAMINE

ME!" This guy goes to the head of the class as <u>the worst evaluator they ever provided me</u>.

Because of a comedy of examiner errors causing the need for repeated evaluations, it took many years to finally settle my claim; seven years to be exact. I call it job security; what else?

Subsequent numerous evaluations took place over seven years for them to finally realize that I was a 100% disabled veteran. I have irrefutable documentation in my three-foot-high stack of reports that substantiate how ill-equipped the VA was in conducting veteran evaluations and the processing of claims. While processing a claim through the VA was a pitiful experience, I need to give credit in an area where the VA does excel. When it comes to medical care for veterans, they do a terrific flawless job; once you get in for an appointment. Oh well, nothing is perfect.

This is a good time to discuss how people like Senator McCain, and other representatives <u>provide assistance to veterans</u> with their disability claims. Prior to the VA finally settling my claim, for years, I would send requests for help to congress and my senatorial representatives. All I ever got from any of them, especially Senator McCain, was a <u>form letter</u> that one of his clerks sends out, indicating that they would look into the matter; that was <u>step one</u>. <u>Step two</u> was a <u>generic inquiry form letter</u> that the representative's <u>clerk sends out to the VA</u>. <u>Step three</u> was, the VA then comes back to the representative and says, "<u>Thank you for the inquiry on Chief Master Sergeant Berry.</u>

Be assured that we are currently working on his claim." Then, the final step, Step 4 is a letter from McCain back to the veteran with a copy of the letter from the VA, stating, "I have been assured that your claim is in the system and working". Well holy shit; I already knew it was in the system, because I put it there, but knew that IT WAS NOT WORKING!" This is the help I sought, to find out why it was dying in the system and never coming to conclusion! All congressional and senatorial inquiries follow the same routine. They are NOTHING, and they do NOTHING; so why don't we get these representatives off their asses, and REQUIRE THEM to actually perform a meaningful task with teeth? The VA should be required to give REASONS to the representative that thoroughly explain why veteran's claims are swept under the rug in this manner, and the representatives must be required to give a full accounting to the veteran. Legislation covering these blatant weaknesses needs to take place! THIS OBVIOUS BEAURACRACY IS WHY THE SYSTEM DOES NOT WORK FOR OUR VETERANS! A constituent is like a person in a row boat in a stormy sea without oars. We know he is there, we know the boat is floating, and someday we might find out whether or not the boat ever got to shore! And in this situation, you can count on your representatives to say, "WE ARE AWARE OF YOUR SITUATION, AND FEEL CONFIDENT THAT YOU MIGHT FIND LAND SOMEDAY." They need to send out the Coast Guard to rescue us, as an analogy. The only real effort by any Senator was the effort I related to about Representative Sanford D. Bishop, getting a bill passed to stop making veterans pay for their own disability. The government's take on that procedure was that they were doing you a favor as the $640 they paid <u>from your retirement</u>, became a non-taxable gift, but you actually were paying for your own disability!

When I was on active duty, when a congressional inquiry came into the base, the very same procedures took place. These inquiries were a joke because they had no teeth, <u>and we knew it</u>. Therefore, in essence, I contend that these inquiries are phony, and serve no purpose, except **to give a veteran false hope**, and should be thoroughly investigated with a view toward eliminating them or giving representatives teeth to scare the shit out of the Veterans Administration. Right now, **no teeth; no scare!** Senatorial and Congressional inquiries are considered one of the government's best jokes as they do absolutely nothing to solve a veteran's problem; absolutely nothing! What a ridiculous system to serve a constituent. Do we really need representatives? Years ago, these elected officials requested assistance so that they would be able to expedite veterans' claims. They received a secretary and an administrator. The administrator sends out the letters I referred to, which are typed by the secretary. Bureaucracy is almost impossible to eliminate from our government.

Now let's cover some of the <u>ongoing waste</u> that I eluded to earlier. When I was stationed at Williams Air Force Base in Arizona, the end of our fiscal year was two days away. Our boss wanted to have the same funds allocation for supplies for the next fiscal year. He cleverly figured out that if we spent less, our fund allocation for the next year would be no higher than what we had spent in the current fiscal year. To overcome this, he had each of his divisions get down to base supply to purchase supplies. It didn't matter what supplies you bought, whether it was mops, pens, pads, or whatever. He gave my section, the Officer's Club, a figure of $1200 to spend for supplies that I didn't need. This was not the only base where this practice was occasioned. It happened every year at every base I was ever assigned. Across the board, this kind of hanky panky throughout the military must be in the billions of wasted dollars every fiscal year! It's a practice that has gone on since the beginning of time, and according to reliable sources, it continues to go on.

CHAPTER 9

The Government Accounting Office (GAO) is an independent, <u>supposedly nonpartisan</u> agency that works for Congress and they are a part of the legislative branch of the United States Government. They are called, "<u>the congressional watchdog</u>." They are good at finding that a $12.00 toilet seat, was being bought by the government for $200. They don't know how to investigate the irregularities that I bring out. They are <u>bean counters</u>, not investigators. They do audits of dollars and cents when it comes to the government's purchases, but they do not know how to begin with finding waste that doesn't show up in a bean count. Another wasted expense to the Government is <u>the cost of the GAO</u>! It is a counterproductive agency that has cost more than the alleged waste they think they find! They have grown from 150 to 3300 employees with an <u>annual budget of $557 million</u>, but they are not even remotely aware of where other higher dollar waste is taking place. <u>I possess the secret</u> of the only way to cut waste and spending. <u>REDUCE THE SIZE OF THE FEDERAL GOVERNMENT!</u> Unfortunately, these long-standing government agencies, like the IRS, just go on and on, and grow, and grow. Since the establishment of the IRS, they have issued more than 8500 directives that have buried them so deeply, that they are unable to use their directives effectively. It is common knowledge now, that government <u>waste and</u> <u>inefficiency is rampant!</u> Statistics reveal that <u>51 cents</u> of <u>every tax dollar</u> the government receives, "IS WASTED"! Here is the sad truth; we don't have a clue as to how to cut the government down to a reasonable, usable size. If I were the next president, I would bring my axe and chop, chop, chop. After I save us from all the waste; I'd naturally be impeached. One of the things we need to do is mind our own business and stay the hell out of other countries problems, and stop being the world's protectors. Enough is enough! The best way to stay out of another country's war is, to stay out of it; but we can't stay out of it, can we? So, let's take a look into what we accomplished by getting into the civil war between the north and south; Korea that is! Well, we were able to establish the 38th parallel as a dividing line. Whoopy doo! The 38th parallel was always there! We just agreed that it was a good dividing line. Was this the total extent of our involvement and the killing of our veterans in Korea?

Let's look at another scenario. North and South Korea was really a civil war. It was their war; not ours. We were scared to death that China inspired North Korea, based in Communism, and would cause Communism to overtake the world. So, naturally, under the guise of offering help, we now have a war of the north and south to butt into with a mission to save the south from communism. We didn't really believe that! Americans no longer believe that old threat that Communism will conquer the world, just like we don't believe that alleged weapons of mass destruction are a factor. It was a good excuse to get involved with a war which was thought to somewhat help our economy but actually cost the taxpayers more than it helped, killed our military, and used our weapons that were beginning to rust, and it also became a great testing ground for new weapon technology. Ok, let's put that to bed for now, and go on back to Vietnam.

Vietnam was another <u>north versus the south</u> in a civil war to determine the fate of the country. We couldn't wait to get into that one. Once again, China inspired North Vietnam was based in Communism, thus, we were needed to <u>BUTT IN!</u> Sound like a familiar story? Again, fearing that Communism would <u>conquer the world</u>, which it never has in 1000 years, we joined in the fight to help the south fight the north. Seems like on any continent, the north is always fighting the south, and it seems we favor the weather in the south. While I was in Vietnam, and after talking to Vietnamese who worked on the base, I discovered that they **<u>did not care</u>** whether or not <u>Uncle Ho</u> was going to unite the country under communism. They just wanted to stop fighting each other. They got their wish. They even named Saigon after Ho Chi Min which is now Ho Chi Min City. They are happy, prosperous, and we are even trading with them, just as we are with China. Tourism has flourished in this Communist country. So, it cost us trillions and over 56,000 military lives <u>to accomplish absolutely nothing!</u> **<u>ABSOLUTELY NOTHING</u>**!

What is my point here? Simply that every country can and will flourish without big brother the United States of America "<u>HELPING OUT</u>!" While communism might flourish in Russia, China, Vietnam, or Korea, it will never flourish in countries where communism is not wanted. **<u>Communism will not work in every country.</u>** Let's stop worrying about communism as we have since the early 1940s. And let's stop using that phony scare tactic as a means to generate support from the American people to put boots on the ground or planes in the air as it has not, and never will conquer us. Let's stop using that as an excuse to butt into other countries' dirty linen. We no longer have credibility in the world as concerns our motives to help the world. They are convinced that our involvement is for the purpose of getting a piece of something that we want, that they have, and historically, has proven to be true. Americans are sick and tired of it all! We have too much work to do at home, as American workers suffer from outsourcing and Off-shoring American products. We shipped Electrolux from Michigan to Juarez, Mexico! Hell, Electrolux was an American tradition! Not only do we suffer the loss of jobs in the United States from outsourcing, but manufacturing opportunities are sent elsewhere. Let's discuss Off-shoring. It is when countries send knowledge-based and manufacturing work to third-party firms in other nations. This then is all about lower wages and lower operating costs. It is really all about "RICH AMERICAN'S GETTING RICHER". On the other hand, Out-sourcing differs in that its concept calls for the hiring of an outside company to perform tasks that would otherwise be performed internally by a company. Let's make this simple by putting some simple math into the equation. Big brand name companies that employ a fifth of all American workers have cut their work force in the United States by 2.9 million during the 2000s while increasing overseas employment by 2.4 million. (This comes from American progress. org).

We need to bring it all back where it was when we were stable and prosperous. At the writing of this book, a presidential candidate, Donald Trump, suggested that to bring it all back into our country we need to charge huge tariffs when the goods come back from foreign countries that should never have left the United States. He threatens that, "when I am President" it will happen exactly this way until companies wise up and get back to putting our people to work. It sounds good. Will it solve the problem? Trump promises that it will. Most people say he will never be elected. I say his chances are better than any of the other republican candidates and predict that he is the only Republican candidate that can beat Hillary Clinton in the final election.

CHAPTER 10

Let's get rid of the Doom and Gloom for a bit, and resort to things that had a positive effect on World War II. Hands down, one of the greatest assets, or perhaps the greatest asset of the Pacific war was the "Code Talkers." The Code Talkers were Navajos. During the war in the Pacific side of the conflict, the Code Talkers drove the Japanese crazy. The Japanese expert code breakers did not believe the sounds they were hearing, and eventually gave up on trying to interpret and break this code of the Navajos. Most Marine officers felt that the Navajos would not fit in with the Marine style of discipline, however; they later learned that while their training at Camp Pendleton at Oceanside, California, was tough, they quickly discovered that the Navajos marched well in cadence, obeyed orders to the T, and their quarters were kept spick and span. It is well documented, that during a dress parade on a miserably hot day, several non-Indian Marines passed out from the heat, while the Navajos, who lived in the Southwest, remained erect information remaining at attention. It took Combat to prove to the doubting officers that the Navajos were not only reliable, but as good a Marine as any of the non-Indian men. In jungle combat, the Navajos proved their ingenuity, scouting and tracking ability, and withstood hardships as good, if not better, then the other men. They proved their value over and over again at places like, Okinawa, The Solomon's, The Marianas, Peleliu, and Iwo Jima.

As a matter of fact, Major Howard Conner, the Fifth Marine Division's Signal Officer said that "The entire operation was directed by Navajo code as they sent over 800 messages without an error. While we talk about our current day PTSD associated with our returning military from combat deployment, there was no evidence of serious psychological problems or combat fatigue among the returning Navajo veterans. Their return to life on the reservation after the war was, however, difficult in terms of them readjusting to reservation life. When questioned about the difficulty in returning to life on the reservation, the majority said that excitement and challenges were missing. Most adjusted rather well by joining the Bureau of Indian Affairs', taking high school classes, and enrolling in colleges under the GI Bill. God Bless the Code Talkers!

Many historians disagree on the issue of, if there was, in fact, a real turning point of the war, what was it, and when and how did it occur. Some believe that it was when the Germans got all the way to Stalingrad, then had to retreat all the way back to Germany. Some opine that it happened when Germany defeated France. I personally agree with those who say that since there were two different enemies, there really can't be a single turning point of World War II. On my own, however, I contend that every battle was some kind of a turning point where we either won or lost. We lost at Pearl Harbor, we lost in the Philippines, for example, and we won at Midway, Okinawa, Tarawa, Iwo Jima, and many other Atolls where we ousted the Japanese. It, therefore, becomes rather difficult to accurately choose **THE DEFINING TURNING POINT OF WWII**. Every damn battle was a sort of turning point. I suppose the historians need something to argue about; and it does not matter because what does, and did matter, was that the Allies won the war! Operation Overlord was the plan of the Normandy landings in June of 1944. Within two months we had more than 3 million allied troops with boots on the ground in France. By September of 1944, the allies were approaching the German border. Within a year, Germany would surrender. Somebody did something right, but nevertheless, we paid the price for numerous **BLUNDERS** along the way.

Let's cover a little bit more waste that my book title references. Let's discuss the F-35 Fighter. **Chuck Yeager**, who is commonly referred to as, **"America's Test Pilot"** says, flatly, that the F-35 is a waste of money! Well, that's just one man's opinion, but this is one man who has the proper credentials to make such a bold statement. Chuck states, "Give me an F-15, which is less than a third the cost, and it will do the job!" Now here comes the clincher; the military has committed to 2500 of these fighters and represents an investment of **$400 BILLION DOLLARS!** Currently this is the only JET FIGHTER THAT CAN NOT FIGHT, AND CAN NOT FLY IN CLOUDY WEATHER! What????? Not only can it not fly in cloudy weather, but it can only fly when it is sunny! Oh, almost forgot; IT CAN'T FLY AT NIGHT! Oh, I left something else out? If there is lightning, it has to be grounded. IN OTHER WORDS, THE DAMN AIRPLANE ISN'T EVEN CLOSE TO BEING FULLY OPERATIONAL at this writing! As a side note, Lockheed, which is the builder of the F-35 had to be bailed out in 1971, being the first big bailout in America, which should have **told us something**; but it didn't. What in the hell are you doing Uncle Sam? Maybe I left out the most important element besides the cost. **AT THIS POINT, THE WEAPON SYSTEM in the F-35 IS FAULTY, BUT IT IS BEING WORKED ON; HALLELUJAH!** Who the hell approves these expenditures? I think Uncle Sam needs a checkbook showing the balance before writing a check. Americans must, or they go to jail. Is there some way that we can put the government in jail for this offense? Too bad!

I keep reading now in 2016. Where the government has an **18 trillion dollar deficit.** Well, to straighten this lie out, as of this very day, 29 October 2016, **the debt is 23 trillion dollars**. Somebody was sweeping a measly 5 trillion under the rug. Or well; chicken feed! Government waste is a real joke. Here is a simple example of waste. In 2012, the U.S. paid an Afghan construction company $500,000 to build an Afghan police training center that began to disintegrate in the rain four months after the project was completed. Again: chicken feed!

An alleged nonprofit contractor billed the U.S. for International Development to the tune of 1.1 million dollars. The International Development turned out to be **PARTIES AND RETREATS** at the height of the Iraq and Afghanistan wars. This was discovered and reported by the Washington Post after their extensive investigation.

Here is another beauty. 6.5 million active Social Security numbers belong to people who must be at least 112 years old and most likely deceased, which certainly puts the government at risk of more fraud and more waste. Nearly 67,000 Social Security numbers have been used in recent years to report wages for people other than the actual cardholders, and the cost of this is about 3 billion in earnings between 2006 and 2011. It's so stupid, it's almost funny!

The IRS is **expertise at going after the little guy**, who I call the **PO FOLKS**, and since they are so good at that, why don't we do away with them as tax chasers, pay an appropriate flat tax, and perhaps put them to work to find all of the actual waste and fraud as described above, since the GAO doesn't know how to do it?

The time has come for Americans to disband the idea that we are the richest country in the world (with the poorest people, by the way) while sitting on their hands, and rather, we should admit that we are rapidly going down the tubes. We need to stand for something to get the show back on the road, which I know we can, collectively. This book is my contribution toward that end. Forget about most of your senators and congressmen as they are brain dead and have no clue what to do, as they are forever on the move for assuring their re-election. Like the Music Man said, "There's trouble in River City"!

At this point in my book, it must be obvious that I am a bitter and concerned American. As a former 27-year career Chief

Master Sergeant of the U.S. Air Force, my comments concerning Generals and the Officer Corps as a whole, might seem rather strong as well. They are strong, and with good foundations for my expressed comments. I just want it fixed; that's all! I wish I could say that I have confidence that it can and will be fixed, but presently, I can only hope for this end. If bureaucracy could win wars, America would never be defeated until the end of time, as no other country is as strong in bureaucracy as the good old USA. This is why it is hard to get through to the brain dead in Washington. The system is so flawed that it takes newly elected congressmen and women, and senators, their first full term before they can even get a handle on what the hell they are doing, or what the hell they are supposed to be doing; then once they learn their jobs, they have to learn how to plow through the bureaucracy, which is almost an impossible mission. The games they play in Washington with Filibusters, and funding delays right down to the last day of a fiscal year is rather childish. The fight between the two parties is disgusting, as their missions seem to be to support their party structure beliefs rather than <u>what is best for the country</u>. Yes, they talk about bypartisanship, but it's only talking. They have learned to distrust each other and that too is childish. Yes, we, the American people are supposed to be the solutions, but we don't have the answers. Voting for the best choice went out with high button shoes because we are enlightened by the press as to who is the best choice. So rather, we are not the solutions; as we have become the problems. I know; that's kind of heavy but do the best you can with it. Basically, two parties with opposite views on how the government should be run do not represent the majority of what the people at large want for themselves and America. Believe it or not, you will not find anywhere in the constitution where there is even a hint of a two-party system. The founding fathers actually preferred a presidential election in which whoever got the most number of votes became President, and the one who got the second most votes became vice president. Pretty simple. Accordingly, why do we now decide that the founding fathers were wrong with that concept?

Now the question on whether or not the Electoral College voting process is fair, proper, adequate, or even a democratic process, is certainly in question. In reality, the winner of the popular vote represents the voice of the American voters, which the Electoral College negates, diminishing the importance for any American to bother to vote since a voter's selection is cast aside. It further distorts governance, in general, thereby distorting the one-person principle of democracy, because electoral votes are not distributed according to population. To receive an electoral vote for each member of its delegation of the House of Representatives is rather bogus and unfair, resulting in a distortion of smaller states in the college. According to a 2010 census, and the number of house seats based on that census, an individual in Wyoming has more than triple the weight in electoral votes than an individual in California. The college also has the potential of causing a 269 to 269 tie vote! And finally, it conveniently makes it virtually impossible for third parties to win elections. In the previous 56 presidential elections, there were four times where **the loser had the most**

votes. To me, this is rather stupid. Therefore, since my single vote does not count, I'm not voting again until it does count. While America is still the greatest country in the world, it can even be greater if the two-party systems die a natural death together with the Electoral College.

Here we are now in 2016, looking at the upcoming election in the next 80 days. To say that it has been an amusing transition from candidates trying to be their party's nominee, to the two nominees now vying for the presidency, would be an understatement. The squabbling between the two candidates has been very entertaining, but we are now at the crossroads of deciding who the biggest liar is, or should I say, who the most convincing liar of the two is. Or, is somebody not lying at all. In all probability, this book will not be published before the election, so I shall make my predictions now, and we shall see how it pans out.

If we look at the polls, we tend to interpret who the winner will be. The problem with the polls is that they represent what the pollsters want them to represent. For example, if Pollsters want the Democratic nominee to look bad, they take a poll in a known Republican area and canvass about 1000 people. The answers will always show that the Democrat is in trouble, for obvious reasons. Polls are a waste, and technically, they become fraudulent when interpreted by the media. They are not representative of anything of substance, and here is why. There are usually 129 million voters as was the case in 2012. Polls of insignificant numbers that are not representative of those 129 million voters prove absolutely nothing. <u>Nobody knows</u> how the 129 million voters will vote.

Hillary Clinton is being called "Lying Hillary" by Trump. Hillary has had several labels for Donald as well, but none as significant as "Lying Hillary". Do candidates lie? Not really; they just distort the truth. The cleverest way to distort the truth is to take a simple statement and call it what it isn't. Here is an example. Hillary said that half of Trump's supporters fit in a basket of "deplorables", calling them racist, sexists, homophobic or xenophobic. She later apologized for that comment. Trump stated that "illegal Mexicans are criminals". This was then quoted by Clinton as Trump saying that Mexicans are criminals, when in fact he said: "illegal Mexicans" are criminals; not all Mexicans. There are far too many accusations to portray the candidate's mudslinging at each other. It is significant, and it is funny at the same time. The name-calling is over, and the voting is about to begin. I have a prediction. Hillary will win. Well, not really. She will win the popular vote. I say this with firm conviction because of the places that she put the greatest emphasis on during her campaign. I believe that she is too busy trying to get a woman vote. On the other hand, Trump, the shrewd guy that we all know he is, has a bigger fish to fry. Understanding the Electoral College, and having a close eye on where Hillary is campaigning, it appears that he will go for the Electoral College for a victory. This is somewhat risky and can backfire, but he is a gamester and has an agenda that nobody can alter. Good luck Mr. Trump. I personally believe that we need his fresh look at how we can make the country great again, which was his slogan of the campaign.

While this book will not be published before the election, it is my intent to spend as much of what I have written thus far to the swamp in Washington, Mr. Trump, The Congress, and the Senate. I feel that it is imperative that they truly become aware of the Blunders and Waste, and I am confident they know very little of what I have addressed as concerns my personal observance of waste and blunders during my 27-year tour of duty, and my disdain for the commissioned ranks of our military forces.

When writing a book, it is often believed that an author sits down at one long session and completes the manuscript. Well, it doesn't work quite that way. For example, my previously published book, 'HOBOKEN, THE LAND OF PLENTY', took around 30 years to complete. This book has been in progress for at least 3 years thus far, and heaven only knows when it will be completed. This is the reason that I have decided to send out a portion of my manuscript before publication, to those parties I mentioned earlier.

CHAPTER 11

Well, it is now April 27th, 2017. The election is over. Trump won by Electoral College as I predicted, and Hillary had the most votes. Wow! What a genius I am! Well, Trump has just completed his first 100 days as President, and while the right clearly portrays his accomplishments, the left tears down his accomplishments and calls them disasters and makes strong pleas for his impeachment. What a joke the Democrats and the left have become. It appears that the jolt of Hillary losing has put them into a state of shock which they are unable to recover from. They are losing credibility with each passing day, as the negativity seems never ending. Oh, my God! He is now the President! As Americans, it is our duty to unite and support his efforts unless he gives us reason not to. I'm having great difficulty with the embarrassment the Democrats are causing as they try to shoot down everything Trump proposes. It is so obvious! I belong to no party. As a matter of fact, I detest the party system as it hampers every move that the other party makes. It's a childish game they play, as is the filibuster routine they practice to stopping the other party from speaking. This should be construed legally as, "The denial of one's right to speak", but it is an acceptable practice instead.

So now, you have seen me commit to not being affiliated with any party as I truly believe that parties obstruct the smooth flow of Government business, refusing to vote because my vote does not count under the Electoral College system, condemning the filibuster movements, telling you that Jane Fonda had a point but made her point at the wrong location, and, surprisingly, telling you that the commissioned officer ranks of the military are shameful, while finally exposing the Waste that is rampant throughout the military system.

Your biggest surprise at this point might be, "How can a 27-year veteran of the U.S. Air Force, hold his disdain for Commissioned Officers of the highest rank?" "Was he a dedicated military man while on active duty?" "Did he follow orders from his superiors?" And, I'm sure you might have several other puzzling thoughts about this veteran. Let me put your minds at ease. I love my country. Even at my current age of 85 years, I would go back into the military if my country needed me. As a military veteran, it was not my place to evaluate orders, or question assigned missions. However, now that I am your typical American citizen, I have the luxury to address all those things that brought me heartburn during my career.

I'm tired of the disgrace that high-ranking officers continue to bring to the officer corps. In this writing, General Wayne Grigsby goes from a two-star to a one-star for his inappropriate relationship with a female captain. <u>When does this shit stop</u>? I know humans thrive on sex, but inappropriate sex has gone rampant with our higher-ranking officers. Hell, let us not forget President Clinton and his friend Monica. Man; right in the friggin White House! You know, what this all boils down to be that sex makes the world go round, and round, and round!

www.ingramcontent.com/pod-product-compliance
Lightning Source LLC
LaVergne TN
LVHW011951070526
838202LV00054B/4889